JUSTICE AND LOYALTY

INTERNATIONAL THEOLOGICAL COMMENTARY

Fredrick Carlson Holmgren and George A. F. Knight
General Editors

Volumes now available

Genesis 1–11: From Eden to Babel
by Donald E. Gowan

Joshua: Inheriting the Land
by E. John Hamlin

Ezra and Nehemiah: Israel Alive Again
by Fredrick Carlson Holmgren

Song of Songs and Jonah: Revelation of God
by George A. F. Knight
and Friedemann W. Golka

Isaiah 40–55: Servant Theology
by George A. F. Knight

Isaiah 56–66: The New Israel
by George A. F. Knight

Jeremiah 1–25: To Pluck Up, To Tear Down
by Walter Brueggemann

Daniel: Signs and Wonders
by Robert A. Anderson

Joel and Malachi: A Promise of Hope, A Call to Obedience
by Graham S. Ogden
and Richard R. Deutsch

Amos and Lamentations: God's People in Crisis
by Robert Martin-Achard
and S. Paul Re'emi

Micah: Justice and Loyalty
by Juan I. Alfaro

Nahum, Obadiah, and Esther: Israel among the Nations
by Richard J. Coggins
and S. Paul Re'emi

Habakkuk and Zephaniah: Wrath and Mercy
by Mária Eszenyei Széles

Haggai and Zechariah: Rebuilding with Hope
by Carroll Stuhlmueller, C.P.

Forthcoming in 1989

Isaiah 1–39
by S. H. Widyapranawa

Hosea
by H. D. Beeby

JUSTICE AND LOYALTY

A Commentary on the Book of

Micah

JUAN I. ALFARO

WM. B. EERDMANS PUBLISHING CO., GRAND RAPIDS

THE HANDSEL PRESS LTD., EDINBURGH

To Fr. Gustavo Gutierrez
on his 60th Birthday

Copyright © 1989 by Wm. B. Eerdmans Publishing Company
First published 1989 by William B. Eerdmans Publishing Company,
255 Jefferson Ave. S.E., Grand Rapids, Mich. 49503
and
The Handsel Press Limited
33 Montgomery Street, Edinburgh EH7 5JX

Library of Congress Cataloging-in-Publication Data

Alfaro, Juan I., 1938-
Justice and loyalty: a commentary on the Book of Micah / Juan I. Alfaro
p.   cm.   — (International theological commentary)
Bibliography: p. 84
ISBN 0-8028-0431-4
1. Bible. O.T. Micah—Commentaries. I. Bible. O.T. Micah.
English. 1989. II. Title. III. Series.
BS1615.3.A54   1989
224′.9307—dc19   88-37084
                                                                        CIP

Handsel ISBN   0 905312 92 9

CONTENTS

EDITORS' PREFACE

The Old Testament alive in the Church: this is the goal of the *International Theological Commentary*. Arising out of changing, unsettled times, this Scripture speaks with an authentic voice to our own troubled world. It witnesses to God's ongoing purpose and to his caring presence in the universe without ignoring those experiences of life that cause one to question his existence and love. This commentary series is written by front-rank scholars who treasure the life of faith.

Addressed to ministers and Christian educators, the *International Theological Commentary* moves beyond the usual critical-historical approach to the Bible and offers a *theological* interpretation of the Hebrew text. Thus, engaging larger textual units of the biblical writings, the authors of these volumes assist the reader in the appreciation of the theology underlying the text as well as its place in the thought of the Hebrew Scriptures. But more, since the Bible is the book of the believing community, its text has acquired ever more meaning through an ongoing interpretation. This growth of interpretation may be found both within the Bible itself and in the continuing scholarship of the Church.

Contributors to the *International Theological Commentary* are Christians—persons who affirm the witness of the New Testament concerning Jesus Christ. For Christians, the Bible is *one* Scripture containing the Old and New Testaments. For this reason, a commentary on the Old Testament may not ignore the second part of the canon, namely, the New Testament.

Since its beginning, the Church has recognized a special relationship between the two Testaments. But the precise character of this bond has been difficult to define. Thousands of books and articles have discussed the issue. The diversity of views represented in these publications makes us aware that the Church is not of one mind in expressing the "how" of this relationship. The authors of this commentary share a developing consensus that any serious explanation of the Old Testament's relationship to the New will uphold the integrity of the Old Testament. Even though Christianity is rooted in the soil of the Hebrew Scriptures, the biblical interpreter must take care lest he "christianize" these Scriptures.

Authors writing in this commentary will, no doubt, hold varied views concerning *how* the Old Testament relates to the New. No attempt has been made to dictate one viewpoint in this matter. With the whole Church, we are convinced that the relationship between the two Testaments is real and substantial. But we recognize also the diversity of opinions among Christian scholars when they attempt to articulate fully the nature of this relationship.

In addition to the Christian Church, there exists another people for whom the Old Testament is important, namely, the Jewish community. Both Jews and Christians claim the Hebrew Bible as Scripture. Jews believe that the basic teachings of this Scripture point toward, and are developed by, the Talmud, which assumed its present form about A.D. 500. On the other hand, Christians hold that the Old Testament finds its fulfillment in the New Testament. The Hebrew Bible, therefore, belongs to both the Church and the Synagogue.

Recent studies have demonstrated how profoundly early Christianity reflects a Jewish character. This fact is not surprising because the Christian movement arose out of the context of first-century Judaism. Further, Jesus himself was Jewish, as were the first Christians. It is to be expected, therefore, that Jewish and Christian interpretations of the Hebrew Bible will reveal similarities *and* disparities. Such is the case. The authors of the *International Theological Commentary* will refer to the various Jewish traditions that they consider important for an appreciation of the Old Testament text. Such references will enrich our understanding of certain biblical passages and, as an extra gift, offer us insight into the relationship of Judaism to early Christianity.

An important second aspect of the present series is its *international* character. In the past, Western church leaders were considered to be *the* leaders of the Church—at least by those living in the West! The theology and biblical exegesis done by these scholars dominated the thinking of the Church. Most commentaries were produced in the Western world and reflected the lifestyle, needs, and thoughts of its civilization. But the Christian Church is a worldwide community. People who belong to this universal Church reflect differing thoughts, needs, and lifestyles.

Today the fastest growing churches in the world are to be found, not in the West, but in Africa, Indonesia, South America, Korea, Taiwan, and elsewhere. By the end of this century, Christians in these areas will outnumber those who live in the West. In our age, especially, a commentary on the Bible must transcend the parochialism of Western civilization and be sensitive to issues that are the special problems of persons who live outside of the "Christian" West, issues such as race relations, personal survival and fulfillment, liberation, revolution, famine, tyranny, disease, war, the poor, religion and state. Inspired of God, the authors of the Old Testament knew what life is like on the edge of existence. They addressed themselves to everyday people who often faced more than everyday problems. Refusing to limit God to the "spiritual," they portrayed him as one who heard and knew the cries of people in pain (see Exod. 3:7-8). The contributors to the *International Theological Commentary* are persons who prize the writings of these biblical authors as a word of life to our world today. They read the Hebrew Scriptures in the twin contexts of ancient Israel and our modern day.

The scholars selected as contributors underscore the international aspect of the series. Representing very different geographical, ideological, and ecclesiastical backgrounds, they come from over seventeen countries. Besides scholars from such traditional countries as England, Scotland, France, Italy, Switzerland, Canada, New Zealand, Australia, South Africa, and the United States, contributors from the following places are included: Israel, Indonesia, India, Thailand, Singapore, Taiwan, and countries of Eastern Europe. Such diversity makes for richness of thought. Christian scholars living in Buddhist, Muslim, or Socialist lands may be able to offer the World Church insights into the biblical message—insights to which the scholarship of the West could be blind.

The proclamation of the biblical message is the focal concern of the *International Theological Commentary*. Generally speaking, the authors of these commentaries value the historical-critical studies of past scholars, but they are convinced that these studies by themselves are not enough. The Bible is more than an object of critical study; it is the revelation of God. In the written Word, God has disclosed himself and his will to humankind. Our authors see themselves as servants of the Word which, when rightly received, brings *shalom* to both the individual and the community.

Juan Alfaro, O.S.B., was born in Navarre, Spain. He joined the Benedictine Order at the Abbey of Our Lady of Montserrat in Manila, Philippines. He did his doctoral studies in theology at the University of Saint Thomas in Manila and his scriptural studies at the Pontifical Biblical Institute in Rome. After teaching at the Benedictine School in Manila, he went to the Mexican American Cultural Center in San Antonio, Texas, in 1973; he is at present the director of the Pastoral Institute of this Center. He teaches also at the Incarnate Word College Pastoral Institute and the Oblate School of Theology in San Antonio, as well as in several Hispanic pastoral centers in the United States. He has written numerous books and articles for Hispanics in the U.S. and is a lecturer in biblical themes, especially in the U.S. and Mexico.

—GEORGE A. F. KNIGHT
—FREDRICK CARLSON HOLMGREN

AUTHOR'S PREFACE

The aim of this commentary is to present the message of Micah with sound theological ideas which will enrich the lives of believers in general and of pastoral ministers in particular. I accepted writing the present commentary because Micah is the most forceful proponent of the ideals of justice, loyalty, and kindness to which the Mexican American Cultural Center (MACC) has been committed since its foundation in 1972. I realize that, perhaps, I could have been more specific in linking the commentary to issues we are confronting in our world today; but, on the other hand, if one ties a commentary too much to contemporary issues, this procedure dates the commentary. Anyone who has his eyes open to the modern world will see the relevance of Micah and of my comments. I had some obvious difficulties in writing in a language that is not my own and had to borrow the terminology of North American scholars such as Leslie C. Allen, Delbert R. Hillers, James Luther Mays, and others. The insights of many scholars are reflected throughout the work, particularly those of the Spanish-speaking world.

I want to thank my friends at MACC for their encouragement, and especially Sister Dorothy Folliard, O.P., who offered some valuable theological suggestions after reading the manuscript and who helped me to put it in readable American English. I also want to thank George Knight and Fredrick Holmgren, series editors, for their meaningful insights and meticulous analysis of the manuscript.

I dedicate this work to the thousands of students and friends who have passed through MACC, enriching us with their faith, hopes, and support.

—JUAN ALFARO

INTRODUCTION

The book of Micah has a special appeal for those who study the powerlessness of the poor, as well as for some groups within the present-day Liberation Theology movement. This book, as much as some of the other prophetic writings, can be classified as a liberationist work, since as long as oppression has existed there have been accompanying movements that were guided by their own liberation theologies. The name "Liberation Theology" might be new, but the reality it refers to is as old as the Bible itself. Latin American theologians have just pointed out to the Christian world a law of religious dynamism, much as Sir Isaac Newton called attention to and clarified the existence of the law of gravitation. Abraham J. Heschel speaks about doing an exegesis of existence from the divine perspective. This is exactly what Micah did and what Liberation Theology is attempting to do. There were signs of the times, pregnant with meaning, in the social and religious life of Israel, and they had to be exposed and interpreted.

Micah, like many sections of the Bible, has a special appeal for Third World peoples who are struggling to free themselves from the shackles of internal and external oppression. Their personal experience and struggles for liberation enable them to provide us with new insights as they approach the Word of God. It must also be pointed out that the Third World was not born or created in a world conference somewhere in Southeast Asia in the 1950s. The reality of the Third World (i.e., nations dependent on others, whose political, social, and economic future is in the hands of the more powerful ones) was very real for the Israelites of the period of Micah. Their national fortunes seemed to be dependent on the whims and imperialistic aspirations of Assyria; their hopes and aspirations could not be protected by Egypt, and Babylon was still trying to emerge as a world power. The superpowers striving to control the world and the great empires engaged in "world wars" were becoming a reality.

As one of the early prophetic works, Micah lends itself more readily for analysis of the fulfillment of its prophecies. At the outset we must point out the idea of fulfillment which will guide us along our commentary. A prophecy is "fulfilled" when it reaches the goal or produces the fruit intended by God and the prophet. The threats and promises of a prophet are not necessarily fulfilled when the announced "event" takes place, but rather when the listeners pay heed to the prophetic message of change and conversion. As is often stressed, a prophetic perspective and proclamation is one of expectation; a prophecy, more than a prediction, is an affirmation of an expectation; this is why so many "nonfulfilled" prophecies have been preserved; they contain the hope of going beyond the present state of hopelessness, and that hope is always valid.

Prophecies are open-ended and are still being fulfilled every time that listeners believe them and follow their directives. It could be said that Micah's most successful and best fulfilled prophecy was that of Mic. 3:12: *"Therefore because of you Zion shall be plowed as a field; Jerusalem shall become a heap of ruins, and the mountain of the house a wooded height."* The effect of this prophecy is said to have been the conversion of King Hezekiah and of the people of Judah (cf. Jer. 26:19). That was the intended goal of the prophecy, salvation and conversion, rather than a simple prediction of destruction. The fact that the temple was later destroyed added a new dimension to the meaning of the prediction. Every time a prophetic text moves a reader to conversion, it acquires a new meaning and the prophecy is fulfilled again. Prophecies are not dead literary or historical "events," but living and timeless "challenges" to conversion for peoples of all times. Micah, in particular, contains one of those prophetic messages, so clear and transparent, that rather than call for an exegesis of the text it seems to demand a new proclamation filled with the energy, courage, and realism of Micah.

MICAH OF MORESHETH

The word of the LORD that came to Micah of Moresheth in the days of Jotham, Ahaz, and Hezekiah, kings of Judah, which he saw concerning Samaria and Jerusalem. (Mic. 1:1)

2

Micah or Micaiah (cf. Jer. 26:18) is a prophet from the 8th cent. B.C., a contemporary of Isaiah, Hosea, and Amos. Although Micah is counted among the Minor Prophets, the greatness of his message is being increasingly appreciated. His name in Hebrew means "Who is like Yahweh," and he became a fearless defender of God's rights over his people. Micah was born in Moresheth (Mic. 1:14), a small town 40 km. (25 mi.) west of Jerusalem, in the region called the Shephelah in the foothills of Judah, not far from Gath near the border of the Philistines. Within an 11 km. (7 mi.) circle from Moresheth were five fortified towns. Moresheth-gath was also fortified and defended the western approaches to Jerusalem; it was an administrative center often visited by military and court officials from Jerusalem. Micah from Moresheth is not to be identified with another Micah, son of Imlah, who had lived one hundred years before in the northern kingdom of Israel (cf. 1 Kgs. 22:8).

As the inscription of the book states, Micah lived in the days of kings Jotham (ca. 742-735), Ahaz (735-715), and Hezekiah (715-687); he exercised his ministry mainly during the reigns of Ahaz and Hezekiah. Micah has clear affinities with his contemporaries Amos and Isaiah and has even been called "Amos redivivus." His message, however, shows without doubt an individual of independent theological thought and of a fearless personality.

The book of Micah offers no personal data on the prophet, hence authors have felt free to speculate on the subject. Micah's call is not narrated, but there is a confident affirmation of his credentials, namely, his awareness of being moved by the Spirit of the LORD (cf. Mic. 3:8; 7:7). Micah's perspective is God's. He speaks in the name of the LORD and knows he is speaking in God's name. Most authors have traditionally considered Micah to have arisen from humble origins, and for that reason we are told nothing of his father or of his family. A good number of commentators think that Micah must have been a small farmer or cattle raiser. Delbert R. Hillers believes that Micah was a "Prophet of a New Age," belonging to some kind of organized group, as a member or as a leader, striving to construct a more satisfying social order and cultural environment. Hans Walter Wolff, on the other hand, suggests that Micah might have been a relatively important person in his time, possibly one of the elders of Moresheth, who was really troubled by the injustices being inflicted on his poor fellow citizens.

The contents, language, and style of the prophecy suggest that Micah was something more than a farmer or poor citizen from a small village. He was a theologian who had cast his lot with the poor of the land and had become a fearless defender of the rights of the oppressed. He was not a farmer who copied Isaiah or Amos, but one of an ardent temperament who had much to denounce and was not afraid to lose. The fact that his words had an impact on the king and the people, who often had deaf ears for the great Isaiah, points either to Micah's personal importance or to the inner force of his oracles (cf. Jer. 26:16-19). It seems more logical to think of Micah as a priest or a Levite who looked at a situation of oppression from the outside, identifying himself with the plight of the poor.

Micah, like Jeremiah who was a priest, made the cult, the priests, and the false prophets the special target of his attacks, seeing them as partners in the injustices of the political leaders, judges, hoarders, and merchants. His attack against the temple itself was such a blasphemous oracle for his hearers that it would be difficult to imagine it coming out of the mouth of a simple layperson (cf. Mic. 3:12). Micah seems to have been a person not afraid to lose his land, if he had any, but who suffered deeply when he saw how the poor were despoiled. He dreamed often of a future shepherd, since he had a clear vision of what the leaders of the people were supposed to be. Some authors have suggested that Micah's prophecy was used in the temple liturgies in Jerusalem, before or after the Exile, and that in the process of its liturgical usage the book was completed and obtained its present form; if this is true, it would be a further indication of Micah's association with priestly circles.

SOCIOPOLITICAL CONDITIONS
OF THE PERIOD OF MICAH

The kingdoms of Israel and Judah enjoyed an extended period of stability and economic prosperity during the long reigns of Jeroboam II of Israel (786-746 B.C.) and of Uzziah of Judah (767-739). The two kings had ample time to develop and strengthen their internal economies, thanks principally to the weakening of Damascus and the absence of outside pressures on account of the internal problems of Assyria. Uzziah, in particular, saw an opportunity to conquer areas in the Philistine territory, near the border of Egypt, as well as in the Transjordan. He fortified border cities and extended his control of the south with the building of the port of Elath in the deep southern region of Ezion-geber. Jotham, Uzziah's successor, saw the rise of Assyrian power under Tigleth-pileser III (745-727), but still enjoyed a prosperous reign, continuing the works of fortification in the region and the beautification of the capital and its temple (cf. 2 Chr. 27:1-8).

The reign of King Ahaz (735-715) was characterized by weakness, injustice, and corruption. His lack of faith in the LORD and his openness to paganism went against the national spirit of Judah. Ahaz could not well resist by himself the pressures of the neighboring states, Israel and Aram, so he asked for help and protection from the Assyrian king. Judah was liberated from the threats of its neighbors, and the capital of Israel, Samaria, was taken and its inhabitants sent into captivity. For its part, Judah became a vassal state of Assyria, having to pay tribute and accept Assyrian divinities (cf. 2 Kgs. 16:7-8, 17). Ahaz had to struggle for the national survival of the kingdom; the result was national insecurity and an internal struggle for the survival of the fittest. The poor paid the bills in those circumstances. The voice of Micah and his contemporaries became the voice of the old national Yahwistic conscience of the divine Covenant and its obligations towards the poor.

The reign of Hezekiah (715-687) awakened the hopes for national liberation, independence, and glory. Hezekiah tried to save a faltering economy by developing international trade with Assyria as well as with Egypt, which was beginning to emerge as a world power after a long period of internal crisis. He secured the ways of communication passing through Israel and Judah, the King's Highway in Transjordan and the Way of the Sea along the Mediterranean coast. He also standardized weights and measures according to international trade, although locally different measures continued to be used and were a tempting means of abuse and oppression against the poor. Hezekiah continued strengthening and restoring the strongholds of the land. He built waterworks, of which the Siloam tunnel is the best known.

King Hezekiah saw the inevitability of war. The fall of Samaria had been an ominous warning for Jerusalem. Assyrian imperialism and Jewish nationalism, religion, and messianism were bound to clash. At the death of the Assyrian king Sargon II (705), Hezekiah tried to evade the Assyrian yoke by joining a general coalition of Palestinian states in open rebellion. This brought upon Judah the wrath of the new king, Sennacherib, who in 701 laid siege to Jerusalem. Hezekiah saved his throne at the price of a heavy tribute and the loss of territory to the Philistines.

The tense international situation of Micah's time resulted in a more serious internal tension within Judah. The denunciations of Micah reflect more accurately the social situation during King Ahaz' reign. Things did not improve much under Hezekiah, in spite of his efforts at reform (which had less to do with social change than with the reformation of the nation's ritual and religious traditions). Assyrian exactions of tribute had aggravated the situation and were a permanent drain on the economy. The poor were always the ones to carry the weight of the new loads. The official religion of the temple at Jerusalem seemed to lack the power to stop and rebuke the blatant injustices. The old moral and social obligations emanating from the Covenant, which had been the bases of society, were increasingly ignored or disregarded.

The economic prosperity under kings Uzziah and Jotham gave rise to a strong current of egotistic materialism. Moral and personal values gradually disintegrated, but the people found comfort in the solemn rites of external religion. Land became the chief commodity for investment of wealth, and soon large estates sprang up all over the land with property passing from the hands of the small landowners to those of the big landholders (cf. Mic. 2:1-5; Isa. 5:8-10). The poor soon became landless, powerless, and voiceless. Corruption was the rule of the day. The powerful took over the fields and homes of the weak, sold the children as slaves, and had no regard for women (cf. Mic. 2:1-11). The political authorities, instead of offering a remedy for the situation, became plunderers themselves, treating the people as if they were sheep for the slaughter (cf. 3:1-4). Judges, priests, and prophets did not condemn the injustices but sold themselves to the system, reflecting well the spirit of the society that fed them (cf. 3:9-11).

Archaeological excavations from this period have not offered proof or confirmed the existence of extreme conditions of wealth and poverty. No ruins of slums have been found; the poor have not left a trace of their existence. Their voice was not heard, for they have always been ignored by human history. Only in the Word of God, especially in Micah's book, are the poor considered for their true worth. After presenting the most pessimistic and dismal picture of a social situation found in the OT, Micah stresses that God has committed himself to the poor and not to the temple or to a city and a dynasty. In his time, Micah was an effective voice for the voiceless.

THE MESSAGE OF MICAH

Although there is a plurality of hands in Micah, the message of the book as it now stands is one of uncompromising doom and total condemnation of the complacency of a nation blindly anchored in a feeling of false security. But Micah looks forward to a hope that history will continue and that God will make a new beginning with his people. Micah's message prodded the national conscience of his period and has continued to influence society whenever social inequities have occurred. By reason of his message and its effects, Micah stands as a major prophet in the history of all humanity.

Micah confronted the external and internal crises that affected the people, pointing out the inner theological connection between the two. Reliance on a foreign power, fortifications, armaments, or idols can never take the place of reliance on the LORD and his Covenant. Reliance on accumulated wealth, unjustly acquired, would prove totally empty; such prosperity was not the result of God's blessing but the fruit of plunder.

Micah, more than any other prophet, shows his concern for the poor and the powerless. He spoke with unrestricted liberty, not being tied to any of the groups or special interests he denounced. Moral corruption and exploitation were the two main sins he continuously denounced. Micah put on parade all the holders of power, declared them guilty of oppressing the poor, and made them targets of his pointed arrows. Micah, like the prophets of his period, saw mainly four groups of powerful persons that were responsible for the unjust social conditions:

(1) Political powers: princes, elders, military officials who exploited the people and used their power to steal and abuse. They were not public servants or shepherds, but wolves tearing apart their victims, the poor common people.

(2) Judicial powers: judges, elders who had made justice a convenient commodity for their enrichment. They did not defend the rights of the poor but sold themselves to the highest bidders.

(3) Religious powers: priests and prophets whose real god was money. With their attitude and for their own interests they had made the temple worship an obstacle to the true conversion of the people. They had led the people to forget that sacrifices and ritual without justice were worthless and could not bring salvation. Liturgical ritual is empty and meaningless unless it is combined with moral integrity and good ethical behavior.

(4) Economic powers: the rich, landowners, hoarders and merchants who deceived, stole, and cheated through every conceivable means, without regard for the most basic rights and dignity of the poor.

Micah, like other contemporary prophets, alternates oracles of doom and denunciation with oracles of hope and salvation. The anger of God will not put an end to his mercy. His loving-kindness, his *hesed* or steadfast love, emanating from his fidelity to the Covenant, will triumph over human wickedness. Salvation depends on the goodness of God, which is assured and eternal. But salvation will come as if *"through fire,"* through a period of judgment, a painful purification, suffering, defeat, and destruction which will do away with the present. The people will have to accept the punishing anger of God, knowing that it is temporary and that it will open the door for a reign of justice. The last word of God will be salvation, but not in the political sense of which the false prophets dreamed.

Salvation will come through a return to Israel's origins, to its humble and lowly beginnings, by laying aside the pride and injustice of Jerusalem. Salvation will not be *from* other nations but *together with* other nations, and it will be a salvation *for* the benefit of all, through a universal peace which still today is the dream of the United Nations:

> . . . and they shall beat their swords into plowshares,
>   and their spears into pruning hooks;
> nation shall not lift up sword against nation,
>   neither shall they learn war any more. (Mic. 4:3)

Salvation will become a magnificent reality when sin will be taken away and annihilated (7:19). All the enemies of God must be eliminated, whether they be idols, armaments, fortifications, or diviners, because in the last instance the enemies of God are the real enemies of the people (5:10-15). The prophecies of salvation of Micah were an important part in the hope and prayer life of the people (7:14-17).

The Unity and Structure of Micah

Micah has been closely linked with Isaiah, since they both share in the same sociopolitical framework, belonging to the same period and region. Recently investigations on Micah seem to have followed in the footsteps of those of Isaiah; authors have begun to speak of a Deutero-Micah, and some even mention a Third Micah. But as Bruce Vawter writes, it is doubtful that any prophet ever wrote, or wrote very much; the prophetic writings we have are the result of later reportage. No single book is the work or derives from the work of any one prophetic genius; all of them are works of redaction and supplementation from many hands, prophetic or otherwise. A Deutero-Micah might have been a real person, but additional work is better seen as the fruit of centuries of additions to an original core message from Micah of Moresheth.

Commentators generally see in Micah the work of an 8th-cent. B.C. prophet who preached between 725 and 701 and who is responsible for chs. 1–3. Some attribute to him also chs. 6–7, although others, with F. C. Burkitt and A. S. van der Woude, based on good reasoning refer these last two chapters to a contemporary prophet, possibly of the same name, from the northern region of the kingdom of Israel.

The sections commonly ascribed to the original Micah of Moresheth have as a general concern the primacy of social justice. The sections attributed to supplementers and redactors from the period of the Babylonian captivity have a common denominator in regarding the main sin of Judah as infidelity to the LORD and failure in temple worship. Almost everyone agrees that sections of chs. 4–5 and 7 are from the hand of one who flourished in the period of the Exile or after. He stresses the theme of the return of the captives, the reconstruction of Zion, universalism, and concern for all nations. As we shall see in the exegesis of the texts, much of the content of chs. 4–5 can be well understood as coming from Micah's time, although they were organized in their present form by a later redactor.

The opinions of commentators concerning the genesis of the materials in the book of Micah, although they are logical and even likely, have little linguistic and stylistic support. Opinions are often based on historical, religious, and psychological presupposition rather than on hard-core literary and textual evidence. The final redactor of the book gave it such a stylistic and theological unity, by reworking previous materials and getting into their spirit, that it is difficult to reach a sound conclusion on the subject, especially since the text is in such a bad state of transmission. For the purpose of our work and commentary, the message of the book is far more important than the author or authors, so we shall try to stress the unity rather than the diversity of its components.

There is a general consensus in seeing in Micah a double or triple pattern of oracles of doom followed by oracles of hope. Israel and Judah constantly stand between judgment and salvation. It is also accepted that there are good grounds for a threefold division, since chs. 1–3 constitute a homogeneous section, while chs. 4–5 are clearly a distinct unit and chs. 6–7 seem to be the work of a northern hand. However, as we mentioned above, the redactional work points to a higher or greater organization of the materials. It is difficult to accept, as some commentators would have it, that the editor removed the oracles from their original historical setting to create a theological pattern in his message; such an original historical setting probably never existed, and oracles were collected and soon organized for liturgical and religious usage.

The remarkable redactional unity of Micah has been noticed by recent authors, especially by Leslie C. Allen and Luis Alonso-Schökel; these authors have offered rather unique divisions of the contents of Micah, though they differ deeply as to the principle of unity running through the whole book. Allen sees a structural and theological pattern in the text, i.e., alternating oracles of hope with oracles of doom, while Alonso-Schökel stresses the larger theological umbrella covering the whole book.

Allen divides Micah into three parts, each composed of contrasting sections (*The Books of Joel, Obadiah, Jonah and Micah,* 260-61). He sees the book organized along the principle of a concentric chiastic scheme as follows:

    I. Penalty and Promise(1:2–2:13)
        —long doom (1:2–2:11) and short hope (2:12-13)
   II. Hope beyond Affliction (3:1–5:15)
        —long doom (3:12) and short hope (4:15

> —hope for the *remnant* in distress (4:6-8)
>> —long distress and short hope (4:9-10)
>>> —short distress and long hope (4:11-13)
>> —short distress and long hope (5:1-6)
> —hope for the *remnant* with distress allusions (5:7-9)
> —long doom (5:10-14) and short hope (5:15)

III. Grace Triumphant over Sin (6:1–7:20)
> —long doom (6:1–7:7) and short hope (7:8-20)

Allen's division seems impressive and positive, stressing the deep unity of the book as a whole, although small details are not always accounted for. The continued series of contrasts between oracles of doom and hope is well taken, although the "long" and "short" terminology does not seem very apt to describe the reality found in the text. The division Allen places between verses 5:9 and 5:10-15 is not so obvious since they are linked by the same catchword, the "cut off" of the adversaries and of the sources of confidence of Jerusalem (5:9, 10, 11, 12, 13, 15).

One can see that the "center" of Micah's prophecy, in Allen's concentric pattern, is to be found in 4:11-13, an oracle which is attributed to Micah of Moresheth even by some authors who deny to him most of chs. 4–5 (Nowack, Deissler, Weiser). This central oracle possibly referred at first to the threats against Jerusalem deriving from Assyrian power, and it came from the mouths of the false prophets who could use truth and traditional hopes of Israel to deceive. This oracle must have had a renewed significance whenever Jerusalem was in danger from its enemies, such as was the case in the time of Jeremiah and even after the Exile. A basic timeless truth was that God is the real LORD of history and that political superpowers are little more than puppets in his hands.

Alonso-Schökel and José Luis Sicre Diaz have proposed a structure for Micah based on the main theological themes of the book, arranged logically according to a vision of God's relation with Israel that finds numerous echoes in the OT. Contrary to the usual pattern of doom and hope oracles, they see a wider unity linking all the themes and organizing them in two main sections in which the theological outlook is the chief concern of the prophecy

> I. The Theophany and Its Consequences (chs. 1–5)
> The punishing manifestation of God (ch. 1)
>> Repercussions on nature (1:3-4)

Repercussions on Samaria (1:6-7)
Repercussions on Judah (1:8-16)
The justification of the punishment (chs. 2–3)
Denunciations against landholders (2:1-5) and argument with the false prophets (2:6-13).
Denunciations against the authorities (3:1-4) and accusation against the false prophets (3:5-8).
Denunciations against judges, priests, and prophets (3:9-11) and final sentence: The doom of Jerusalem (3:12).
Punishment will be superseded by salvation (chs. 4–5)
In the future and not now (4:1–5:1)
Not from Jerusalem but from Bethlehem (4:8; 5:2-4)
Not cruel but beneficial for all (5:5-9)
Requiring purification (5:10-15)

II. The Judgment of God (chs. 6–7)
Summons and accusation of ingratitude (6:1-5)
Rejection of empty ritual and demand of justice and loyalty (6:6-8)
There is no justice (6:9-16)
There is no loyalty (7:1-6)
Acceptance of divine retribution, acknowledgement of sin, and certainty of pardon (7:7-20)

Alonso-Schökel's division would make both sections of Micah a kind of *rib* or prophetic covenant lawsuit, with a theophany and a judgment, a form often found in the OT (cf. Isa. 1:2-3, 10-20; Hos. 4:1-19; Jer. 2:1-37; Ps. 50:1-23; Deut. 32:1-25). The prophet could be seen as the LORD'S attorney, who knows beforehand the weight of the evidence and the outcome of the trial. The last word of God will be one of pardon and life because of his loving mercy and loyalty.

With some modifications, the division of Micah's book in this commentary will follow the lines of Alonso-Schökel. As we proceed to the Commentary, we would like to point out again that the text of Micah presents serious problems, and that at times it is difficult to translate and understand. The frequent use of wordplays, alliterations, sudden transitions, and rough metaphors adds to the difficulty of the commentator. We shall speak of individual problems and interpretations as we meet them in our Commentary.

THE PUNISHING
MANIFESTATION OF GOD
Micah 1:1-16

The prophecy of Micah opens with a solemn theophany called for by the crimes of Israel and Judah. The consequence will be the immediate punishment of Samaria and the approaching doom of Jerusalem. The scene is one of a "last judgment" which forebodes the end of a historical era, the end of the world of Samaria and the crumbling of the world around Jerusalem. The end of their worlds would be a necessary step for the birth of a new world, for a truly new beginning.

Micah's threat of destruction was clear at a theological level since the injustices of society were calling for a punishing manifestation of God. The threat was becoming historically obvious since the time he started his ministry (ca. 725 B.C.), with the rising imperialistic ambitions of Assyria. The denouement seemed imminent twenty years later, with the prophetic interpretation of the fall of Samaria in 722 becoming a warning and an omen for Jerusalem threatened by the Assyrians.

Some authors think that the first chapter of Micah's prophecy originally referred only to the fall of Samaria, and that the repeated allusions to Judah and Jerusalem (Mic. 1:5, 9, 12, 13) were added later to apply the section to Jerusalem during the period of Sennacherib's invasion. The wrath of God had been kindled principally by the injustices committed against the poor all over the land, especially by the ruling classes living in the capital city, the center of power.

Samaria and Judah, as well as the whole world of nature, will experience the effects of God's manifestation and will be witnesses in the coming judgment (vv. 2-7). Judah, and Jerusalem in particular, will have to learn from the fate of Samaria if it is to avoid a similar fate. Reading the signs of the times, the people have to understand that the historical pressures of the gradual and unavoidable invasion of the neighboring territories are the final theological invitations to a conversion and salvation that are still possible (vv. 8-16). Each social group—the rich, the political and judicial authorities, as well as the religious leaders—will have to face and acknowledge their sins if they are to escape the most dreadful catastrophe (2:1–3:12). The last word from God will be one of hope and salvation, although it will not happen the way the leaders expect it (4:1–5:15).

1   The superscription of the book of Micah is similar to that of other prophets (cf. Isa. 1:1; 2:1; Jer. 1:1-3; Hos. 1:1; Joel 1:1; Amos 1:1; Zeph. 1:1); it was written by the editor or the collector of the oracles. The prophecy is the *Word of the LORD* and is to be recognized and believed as revelation coming from Yahweh. For this very reason it was preserved and was considered valid for all nations and for all times, since the Word of God is eternal. Moresheth-gath, Micah's place of origin, was a small town halfway between Jerusalem and the seacoast, much less prominent than the neighboring fortresses mentioned in the second part of the first chapter. Practically nothing else is said in the book about the person of Micah, since what is important is the message rather than the messenger. The kings of Judah are named because Micah was a prophet of the southern kingdom. Northern Israel no longer exists; therefore Micah lacks any reference to northern monarchs. Although King Jotham is mentioned, no oracle of Micah can be assigned to that early period; most of the oracles find a more appropriate setting during the reign of Hezekiah. Micah *saw* the Word of the LORD, namely, its efficacy and transforming power, as well as its judgment sentence over Samaria and Jerusalem, the two urban centers which had become the symbols of the sins and injustices that afflicted the kingdoms of Israel and Judah.

REACTION OF NATURE TO THE MANIFESTATION OF GOD (1:2-4)

The prophecy opens with a universal invitation to all peoples to listen and be witnesses in the coming judgment. Yahweh stands as LORD of all the nations of the earth. He comes out of his heavenly temple, like a king out of his palace, to render judgment. God is both prosecutor and judge, but he wants the whole world to witness the justice of his procedure and to learn from the process. Ironically, although all nations are invited to the judgment, the name of the accused is not yet revealed. The action of God, though restricted to a small geographical area, has a cosmic stage and background. Nations will witness God's firm demand for justice from the people and persons he has chosen as his own (cf. Amos 1–2). The punishment of Israel and Judah is also to serve as a lesson for other nations (cf. Jer. 25:29).

God presents himself showing his majesty and power in the chastisement of sin, while in the last section of the prophecy the power of God shines in his mercy and compassion (cf. Mic. 7:18-20). Nature, the earth, is presented as a creature that knows its Creator and acknowledges his presence. Often in the OT mountains and rivers exult at the saving presence and actions of Yahweh; the fields sing for joy and rejoice in the abundance of fruits and flowers (cf. Ps. 65:9-13; 96:11-13; Isa. 44:23; Amos 9:13). The sea, together with the rivers and mountains, is also presented as trembling before the mighty actions of God's hand (cf. Ps. 95:5; 114:3-8; Zech. 14:4). Micah condenses elements describing a volcanic eruption and an earthquake to portray the irresistible power of God. The elements of Mic. 1:4 are organized along the lines of an alternating parallelism to heighten the intensity of God's presence:

A   "And the mountains will melt under him
B   and the valleys will be cleft,
C   like wax before the fire,
D   like waters poured down a steep place."

If the mountains and the inanimate creatures recognize the presence of the LORD and melt with fear, what will be the reaction of the people when they see the avenging power of God over them? The sad truth seems to be that all the divine power is incapable of melting the hearts of a recalcitrant, sinful people. But God's avenging power will ultimately be redemptive, resulting in conversion and salvation. All nations and peoples must understand that there is a power in history which comes from beyond human reach and which surpasses all the powers of the universe. In any given moment, that divine power can be made manifest, and can show that human history is in the hands of God and that he is the true ruler and maker of history (cf. vv. 12-15; 4:1-5, 11-13).

REACTION OF SAMARIA TO THE
MANIFESTATION OF GOD (1:5-7)

Micah 1:5 appears to come from the hand of a redactor. The link with the preceding verse is not smooth, and the parallelism of its members does not measure up to the standards of other parallelisms in Micah.

"All this is for the transgression of Jacob
and for the sins of the house of Israel.
What is the transgression of Jacob?
Is it not Samaria?
And what is the sin of the house of Judah?
Is it not Jerusalem?" (1:5)

Because the correspondence of the elements of this verse is not clear, some authors change "Israel" to "Judah", thus obtaining a general accusation at the beginning of the verse which is then detailed in the two following sections. As the text stands, there is the general correspondence "Jacob . . . Israel" and "Jacob/Samaria . . . Judah/Jerusalem." Some consider the references to Judah and Jerusalem as later additions, thinking that in the original text Jacob/Israel was the only party with a double accusation. However, by introducing Jerusalem as a sinful city and so far without punishment, the prophet (or the editor?) creates a suspense in the reader which will be resolved in 3:12 when the punishment of Jerusalem is announced in terms identical to those used in 1:6 for Samaria.

Although the text as it stands is difficult, it reveals the depth of the prophet's conviction as he refers to the temple of Jerusalem as if it were a pagan high place of idolatry. Indeed, the true God is not really worshipped there; Mammon, money, is the real god adored in Jerusalem (cf. 3:8; Isa. 57:11). Samaria and Jerusalem are the two centers of political and religious power that have made for themselves idols out of their own interests. Metropolitan corruption will be at the root of the fall of both kingdoms, for the corruption at the top is filtering down to the lower levels. The two cities are rebellious because they have forgotten their Covenant obligations to their LORD and have sinned by falling short of the moral ideal to which they have been called.

The oracle of Mic. 1:7 dates from around 722 B.C., the year of the fall of Samaria into Assyrian hands. God speaks in the first person, without any introductory formula. Samaria can expect only destruction and desolation from God; the time of judgment has come, and there seems to be no room for repentance. In reality, the Assyrians will not be the ones to destroy Samaria; God himself will destroy that city. Samaria, as dust returns to dust, will return to the pristine status it had before it was built; the place will become again a vineyard, and the city will be condemned to oblivion (cf. 1 Kgs. 21). From the hill on which the city stood, its stones will roll down to the valley, and not a stone will remain upon a stone. The fate of Samaria will be a warning for the inhabitants of Judah and Jerusalem.

The physical ruin of Samaria contemplated in Mic. 1:6 is placed on the same level as its religious devastation described in v. 7. God will destroy the foundations of the houses as well as the images and idols; the physical and the religious ruins are interdependent. God does not admit rivalry and will destroy the idols and everything connected with them. The religious vocabulary of v. 7 might be an allusion to the false, adulterated worship of Yahweh in the northern kingdom, even if it was not practiced in the city of Samaria itself; the analogy of religious prostitution is first found in Hosea and becomes common in the later prophets. Prostitution should be understood metaphorically as infidelity to God, the true spouse of Israel (cf. also John. 4:16-20). In the proper sense of the word, prostitution could be understood literally, for it was practiced in the fertility rites of the Canaanite temples, especially in the northern kingdom. People went to Baal with gifts they believed had been received by worshipping Baal, the god of fertility. Accordingly, Micah proclaims that enemy soldiers will plunder the treasures of the temples and will squander them with prostitutes. Again, like Samaria, her idols will return to the dust from which they came.

Samaria, as a matter of fact, was not destroyed by the Assyrians; but its inhabitants, the living stones, were deported to Assyria and went into the valley of death, never again to return. The word of God became terribly true for the inhabitants of the sinful city.

REACTION OF JUDAH TO THE
MANIFESTATION OF GOD (1:8-16)

The text of the elegy over Judah is in such a poor state of preservation that the various attempts at reconstruction have not found any widespread support. Verses 8-9 form a close unit and serve as a bridge to what follows. They could be viewed as a lament over the fall of Samaria, or as a cry over Judah before the threat of the invasion of King Sennacherib in 705 B.C. Some authors see them in relation to the invasion of Sargon II in 712. Most probably, these two verses serve with v. 16 to bind this section together (i.e., they form what is called an "inclusion," hence the whole section is better seen as an elegy over Judah and Jerusalem.

The prophet brings in a growing choir of neighboring cities to join the lamentation. Only seven of the twelve cities mentioned are known; they are located southwest of Jerusalem, near Micah's birthplace. The elegy of David over Saul and Jonathan (cf. 2 Sam. 1:20) serves as point of reference and inspiration for Micah, probably because it was well known and had become a proverbial expression for national disasters.

Micah shows in this elegy his true function as a prophet. His mission is not simply to announce calamities, but to lead the people to conversion. The prophet, announcing captivity, is himself the first "captive of sorrow" (cf. Isa. 20:2-4). His display of external signs—such as going naked and barefoot, wailing uselessly like animals in the desert at night when no one listens—all point to a captivity coming over the people. The "wound" of Jerusalem, the evil and corruption brought about by blatant injustice, has come to the "gate" of the city, to the center of the political, social, and religious life of the people, to the tribunals of justice. Once justice is so deeply subverted, the situation has no moral solution; the social and religious system is mortally wounded and has to end in death and total destruction (cf. Mic. 3:12).

It is remarkable that the prophet does not call here directly for prayers, repentance, and conversion. The people are so ensnared in injustice that the time for conversion has passed and the hour of judgment is at hand. The time remaining is an evil time; the evil that has come to the "gate" of the capital city will go forth, penetrating everywhere, reaching to the farthest ends of the territory; nothing will be able to stop it until the hand of God will put an end to everything.

As we said above, the text of 1:10-15 is so poorly preserved that it is difficult to make good sense out of it. The prophet names a series of cities, including his own place of origin, Moresheth-gath, resorting to frequent use of paronomasia, trying to draw a tragic meaning from the very name of each city (*nomen—omen*). Something similar was done by his contemporary, Isaiah (cf. Isa. 10:27-32). It is difficult for us to understand in some cases the paronomasia, wordplays, and alliterations used because we are not fully familiar with the geographical location of some of the cities, and especially because we know next to nothing about the historical and social connotations that their names had for the listeners of the prophet. Paronomasia and alliteration were useful tools to keep the message in the memory of the listeners; they have an added effect in a prophecy of doom. In some instances the relationship between the name of the city and the punishment announced is partially clear even to us: Gath—*tagiddu* ('announce'), Beth-leaphrah —*aphar* ('dust, ashes'), Shaphir—*shophar* ('horn'), Zanaan—*yazeah* ('go out'), Lachish — *rekesh* ('chariot'), Moresheth — *meorashah* ('betrothed'), Achzib—*akzab* ('deception'), and Mareshah—*yoresh* ('conqueror, possessor').

Gath was a well-known town on the border of the Philistines. The calamity should not be announced and cries should not be heard in Gath, so that the enemies will not rejoice or derive comfort. In Beth-leaphrah people should roll in the dust and openly express their sorrow, since this city of Benjamin was far from the border and their cry would not be heard by the enemies. Shaphir, the beautiful and shining city ("sapphire"), will become ugly, naked, and full of shame. In Zanaan the inhabitants will be paralyzed with fear; in their sorrow they will stay indoors, as they will be unable to go out to help others or to commiserate with their neighbors. Maroth, the bitter or rebellious city, will be sick. All these cities will react in fear and mourning to the approaching enemy; they will be filled with the confusion of a growing disintegration. In the fight between good and evil, the latter is prevailing and approaching Jerusalem (cf. Mic. 1:12).

Lachish was the fortified city from which the Assyrians proceeded to attack Jerusalem. We do not know the reasons for Micah's specific denunciation, pointing to Lachish as the root and beginning of the sin of Jerusalem and Israel. It could be that Lachish had been a source of idolatry for the region; but, more in accordance with the rest of Micah's outlook, one could better see an allusion to the city's expenditures in arms and fortifications which only served to cover its weakness, to impoverish many, and to create a sense of reliance on its own strength to the exclusion of reliance on God. Israel and Judah had followed the example of Lachish and had not placed their trust in the LORD (cf. 5:11).

Micah 1:14 seems to be a gloss, since it changes in tone from the preceding and serves, apparently, to give clarifications which are equally unclear to us. Moresheth-gath is like a bride being lost or given to another husband; it is a tribute given to a new master. Mareshah will be conquered. The "glory of Israel," its army, as in the days of David (cf. 1 Sam. 22:1) will find refuge in a poor and indigent place, Adullam. Thus, Micah makes an allusion to David at the beginning and at the end of his elegy. History will repeat itself or, rather, will be repeated by God, and once again Israel will lament in poverty and misery. The text of 1 Sam. 22 gives us an inkling into the mood of the prophet in this elegy:

David departed from there and escaped to the cave of Adullam; and when his brothers and all his father's house heard it, they went down there to him. And every one who was in distress, and every one who was in debt, and every one who was discontented, gathered to him; and he became captain over them. (1 Sam. 22:1-2).

The cities that felt secure and prosperous, living in a false peace and tranquility, will end in sorrow and distress.

The elegy concludes in Mic. 1:16 by way of inclusion, with an invitation to express intense sorrow and desperation through the traditional rites: cutting one's hair, a sign of strength and life, and shaving the head (cf. 1 Kgs. 13:30; Jer. 22:18; 34:5).

Why such a dreadful sentence? In the following two chapters, the prophet will specify the crimes of those responsible for the situation: the rich who use foul means to prosper (even at the expense of the poor), the rulers and elders who use their power for the subversion of justice, and the priests and false prophets for whom money is far more important than the service of the LORD.

THE JUSTIFICATION
OF THE PUNISHMENT:
DENUNCIATIONS OF POWER
Micah 2:1–3:12

The punishment announced by Micah in the preceding chapter was well deserved. Micah saw that all persons who hold power were afflicted with the same malady and that there was a common denominator in all the social evils that afflicted the region. All the leaders had fallen into a subtle form of idolatry, to which the prophet had made a veiled allusion in Mic. 1:5. The real god of the existing society was money, Mammon, and everything else was intended for his service; the poor were the main sacrificial victims. All those who had power, whether political, judicial, economic, or religious, used it for evil and for their own advantage. Because values had been perverted, the princes and rulers, the rich, the priests, and false prophets were all guilty and responsible for the religious crisis that had all the seeds for the destruction of that society. The Word of God denouncing them was effectively ignored, and the voice of the true prophets was being contested and silenced. Micah wanted to be heard, even if his listeners had to be forced to hear.

The oracles of chs. 2–3 are considered by some authors as the product of a single ministry of Micah in Jerusalem, during which he was interrupted by his adversaries on two occasions, in 2:6-7 and 12-13. It seems, nevertheless, more in agreement with the rest of the book to consider the oracles as a redactional unit, arranged by a later editor who wanted to portray the dramatic opposition the prophet had to overcome to bring his message across to his listeners.

The denunciations of power open with a direct indictment against landholders (2:1-5); this provokes an argument with Micah's adversaries, the false prophets, who are convinced that God is on their side (vv. 6-7). The prophet denounces them and attacks them (vv. 8-11). There follows an oracle of salvation which is best seen as a response of the adversaries to the threats of Micah

(vv. 12-13); some authors see this salvation oracle as a later editorial addition to soften the impact of the preceding threat. Micah retorts with a stronger and more personalized oracle against the authorities (3:1-4), and with a direct indictment against the false prophets (vv. 5-7). He passes on to stress the contrast between his motivation and purpose and that of his enemies (v. 8). Since Micah is filled with the power and the Spirit of the LORD, he takes on directly all the ruling powers and threatens them with an unheard of calamity, the destruction of Jerusalem and its temple (vv. 9-12).

DENUNCIATIONS AGAINST LANDHOLDERS (2:1-5)

The first half of the 8th cent. B.C. had been a period of relative prosperity, both for Judah and Israel. A rich class had gradually emerged and had come to control the different facets of the people's social life. These riches were conspicuous in the size of the land holdings, in the abundance of cattle, in the splendor of the homes, and in the number of servants and slaves. In his first concrete prophetic indictment Micah takes on the landholders and landgrabbers, the most active and ruthless among the rich.

The taking of other people's land, the "inheritance" of their forefathers, was looked upon as a most execrable crime which deserved the worst of punishments (cf. 1 Kgs. 21). The land had always been considered one of the basic gifts of God for his people, the object of the early promises to Abraham (cf. Gen. 12:1, 7; 13:14-18). Individual Israelites were to see themselves as mere tenants, for God was the only real landlord (cf. Exod. 19:5; Lev. 25:23). The land was to be protected and cared for, so that it could be handed down as a sacred trust from generation to generation. The land, after the Sinaitic legislation, had become the sacrament of the liberation signified and intended by the Exodus from Egypt. It was through the possession of a parcel of land that the individual Israelites were to enjoy liberty, dignity, and sufficiency. A person who lost his or her land, in such an agricultural society, was at the mercy of others; a landless person at times could do no better than to sell herself and her family as slaves in order to survive.

The ownership of the land, of one's "inheritance," had been protected by religious land reform laws, especially by the Jubilee Year legislation, so that families would not be deprived for long from owning their own land. To take the land of a family, as Micah implies, was to create slaves and to destroy effectively the whole plan of salvation intended by God for his people. Thus, landgrabbing came to be considered the worst of threats to the socioreligious system based on the Covenant traditions of Exodus. Landgrabbing became a serious problem in the history of Israel and Judah, as attested by the denunciations we find in Scripture (cf. Isa. 5:8-9; Deut. 27:17; Prov. 23:10-11; Neh. 5:1-3; 1 Sam. 8:11, 14-17; 1 Kgs. 21:1-23). Isaiah and Micah make landgrabbing the first target in a series of various denunciations; Deut. 27:17 puts it at the head of a list of sins against property, after the sins against God and one's own family. Landgrabbing was a capital sin, the root of many other sins and injustices.

The oracle against landgrabbers has two sections, the accusation (Mic. 2:1-2) and the fitting punishment (vv. 3-5). The accusation is presented first in the most general terms (v. 1) and then specified to concrete persons (v. 2); likewise, the judgment and punishment are announced first in general terms (v. 3) and then concretized into the perspective of the landgrabbers themselves (v. 4) and into that of God (v. 5)

Micah starts with a cry of woe which reminds us of the elegies sung over the dead. The landgrabbers are going to receive a death sentence. The accusation is at first generic and imprecise, so as to attract the attention of the listener more effectively and make him wonder whom the prophet has in mind. Micah underlines the covetousness of the rich; it inspires all their works and actions and produces all sorts of injustice; it goes directly against the Tenth Commandment:

> Neither shall you covet your neighbor's wife; and you shall not desire your neighbor's house, his field, or his manservant, or his maidservant, his ox, or his ass, or anything that is your neighbor's. (Deut. 5:21; cf. Exod. 20:17)

There is a system and a process in their wrongdoing: the evil ones plot, plan, and do evil. Their sins are the product of premeditation and not just the result of a sudden and improvised temptation. In their beds they dream of ways and means to increase their holdings, and in the morning work actively to make their dreams come true.

The "reason" for the existing evil is that "it is in the power of their hand." Possibly Micah had in mind the royal officials from

Jerusalem who were assigned to the military fortresses and small towns that surrounded Moresheth, and whose first thought could well have been "What are we in power for?" The text, however, seems to be better adapted to the longtime residents of his hometown whom he knew too well, their dreams and plans included. Power at the service of greed was the root of the evil. Without their power, their greed would have gone unfulfilled. Micah's view of power is not far from that of the evangelist Luke, who puts into the mouth of the devil, tempting Jesus, those terrible words not found in the parallel of Matthew: "To you I will give all this authority and their glory; *for it has been delivered to me, and I give it to whom I will*" (Luke 4:6). Power without love is demonic; power with love is divine, and God ultimately has all power in heaven and on earth. The experience of Micah, as well as of Luke, was that those who had power used it for their own benefit, to satisfy their greed, rather than to be of service and help to others, especially to those in need.

The denunciation of Micah against landgrabbers brings to mind the similar denunciation of Isa. 5:8: "Woe to those who join house to house, who add field to field, until there is no more room, and you are made to dwell alone in the midst of the land." Isaiah presents a concrete accusation with a concrete punishment, stressing the economic aspect of the sin and punishment: they *join* houses and they *add* fields; they will reap economic ruin. Micah, on the other hand, is more intense than Isaiah in stressing the moral aspect of their deeds: they *covet, seize,* and *take away;* they *oppress* a man and his house and inheritance. The punishment for Micah will be a new division of the land in which the hope of the poor will be fulfilled while the rich will be cast away. Micah underlines the human and moral dimension of the crimes; it was not just a question of houses and lands, but one of *people* oppressed, which was far more important. The plight of the innocent victims is in his mind here, and it will be reinforced in another accusation (cf. Mic. 3:1-3) where he will state that the people are treated like sheep for the slaughterhouse.

Micah denounced the landgrabbers who prospered at the expense of the poor. There was poverty in the land, but it was an inflicted and perpetrated poverty. There is no specification of whether the lands were simply taken by force by the royal officials (cf. 1 Sam. 8:14-18) or by unscrupulous creditors who in their own way manipulated the economy, lending to the poor while aiming to take over their fields when they would be unable to pay back their debts. The defense of the rich could well have been that "business is business," but for the prophet, in most cases, that type of business was pure thievery.

The poor were being deprived of their "inheritance," which might refer to their lands; Micah, however, seems to go deeper, thinking of the children of the family who are the most precious inheritance of their parents (cf. Mic. 2:9; Ps. 127:3). The oppression of the parents results in greater oppression for their children, who are deprived of a future.

The calculations and planning of the rich took place at night. Ordinary thieves planned by day and executed at night, but the powerful committed their crimes in broad daylight, either because they were callous and confident that no one would challenge their power or because they had done everything according to the laws that greatly favored them. The poor, totally oppressed, were powerless and voiceless. Micah lifted up his voice in the name of those who were unable or too scared to speak. During the prophet's time it was already clear that the children of the world were more shrewd than the children of the light (cf. Luke 16:8).

Such antisocial conduct of the rich landgrabbers deserved an exemplary punishment from God, one best befitting the crimes. God will measure the persons with the same measures they use for others (cf. Matt. 7:2). The robbers will be robbed; the oppressors will become oppressed. As the rich have plotted evil against the poor, so God has plotted a similar evil against the rich, namely slavery and deprivation of their property. Evil will boomerang on the sinner.

The rich plot evil "because it is in the power of their hand," but when God executes judgment they will be truly powerless and unable to escape. They will learn that history is not the product of human or blind forces, but that it is the power of God which will cause things to happen. When confronted with that divine power, human power becomes impotent.

The rich are said to constitute a "family," a group of gangsters similar to a Mafia family. They form a brotherhood, for they are all sons of evil, and their common bond is the great injustices they perpetrate against the poor and the benefits they reap from them. But God will humiliate them; those who walk proudly, with lifted heads, will walk as prisoners towards slavery in shame (cf. Isa. 9:4; Jer. 27–29). This was a graphic image for the prophet's audience. During Micah's time Assyrian deportations had become common events which sooner or later would reach Jerusalem.

"In that day" designates an indeterminate eschatological future that is sure to come, when God will execute judgment. Then there will be singing; the poor will intone their own Magnificat, when they see the rich go away empty-handed. A taunting satire will be sung against the fallen enemies as they are despoiled and deported (cf. Isa. 14:4; Hab. 2:6). The words of lamentation of the rich will become the joyful song of the poor (Mic. 2:4b,c).

The text of v. 4 is rich in paronomasia and alliteration which serve to reinforce the prophetic thought and to underline the mockery of the rich. The sense seems to be that the rich bewail their lot when they see how they are ruined, how they are deprived of their property, and how their fields are given to the "rebellious" or to the "infidels." The rich have a total disregard for the poor, whom they insult in their language, calling them "infidels." Their way of judging is similar to that of the Pharisees, who branded the simple people who listened and believed in Jesus with an equivalent epithet: "But this crowd, who do not know the law, are accursed" (John 7:49). The rich will consider a national calamity to be the "evil" that will come upon them when lands will be divided again; they consider themselves the people of God, being blinded to the fact that they are the exploiters of the *real* people of God, the poor and the humble. In a parallel way, in our own days, the rich of Third World countries consider it a national calamity when land reform laws are put into effect; they think that their own private interests are identical with the national interests.

The lamentation of the rich is reinforced in Mic. 2:5 by a religious interpretation of the coming event. The future of history belongs to the poor. A new people of God will gather in cultic assembly, and the rich and the landgrabbers will be excluded. The text alludes to the traditions of the conquest and distribution of the land by Joshua, using sacred lots, for the land was a gift from God (cf. Josh. 14:5; 18:8-10; 19:51; Num. 33:54; 34:13). Probably there was a periodic redistribution of lands in Israel each Sabbatical Year, as well as a general land reform prescribed for the Jubilee Year. The land was again distributed to the families according to an ancient custom. Thus the psalmist could rejoice and praise God for his good luck in the distribution: "The lines have fallen for me in pleasant places; yea, I have a goodly heritage" (Ps. 16:6). Psalm 37 expands the hope expressed by Micah that in the future assembly of the LORD those now oppressed, the meek and humble, will inherit the land while the rich will be utterly ruined, excommunicated from the chosen people of God.

Some consider Mic. 2:5 a later addition; its prosaic character and terminology seem to point to a postexilic Priestly hand; the last words, "in the assembly of the LORD," seem to break the rhythm. It could be that only the last words are an addition; but whichever the case, the verse does not contradict the preceding one but rather stresses and underlines the religious meaning of the coming punishment.

ARGUMENT WITH THE FALSE PROPHETS (2:6-13)

After the denunciations of the rich landholders and landgrabbers, Micah adds a dialogue with the false prophets. These men have become the voice of the rich and the powerful, while the true prophet remains the voice of God, the defender of the rights of the poor.

Micah 2:6-7 seem to contain an objection to the preceding oracle of denunciation and doom. We see in them a series of rhetorical questions from the offended parties, beginning with an elegant, though enigmatic, paronomasia (v. 6). The text of this section is difficult and poorly preserved, filled with textual difficulties and with allusions to events about which we know very little. There are clearer sections that give us a clue to understanding the more obscure ones; one key to the understanding of the text is the various meanings of the verb *nataph,* namely, "to drop," "let drop," "drip," "let fall" (sentiments, prophetic declarations), "flow," "pour," "speak," "preach," "prophesy" (cf. vv. 6, 11). The enemies try to devalue Micah's message, and the prophet repays them in the same coin, calling them spiritual charlatans.

Micah finds himself with people interested in silencing his prophetic activity or at least in rendering it harmless and without prestige. He realizes that silence is the arm of the rich, inasmuch as they want to create silent majorities whose voices will not be raised and heard so that their oppression will go unchallenged. The spiritual defenders of the rich, the false prophets, will go farther, putting truth aside and substituting for it false truths, since their interest lies in defending the "peace" of the status quo and in gaining economic advantage (cf. 3:5, 11).

The rich do not like to hear about "ugly" things, since for them the status quo is beautiful. In their opinion, the prophet should not speak of such areas as politics or the economy, but must limit himself to speak of a lofty God, far above the earthly cares of this world; he should speak about the good things of life, such as wine (cf. 2:11). Contemporary prophets, especially Amos and Isaiah (cf. Amos 7:10-17; Isa. 30:8-11; Jer. 26:9ff.; 1 Kgs. 18:10; 19:2; 22:8), had to fight against similar efforts to silence them, and they reacted strongly with added denunciations:

> And now, go, write it before them on a tablet,
>   and inscribe it in a book,
> that it may be for the time to come
>   as a witness for ever.
> For they are a rebellious people,
>   lying sons,
> sons who will not hear
>   the instruction of the LORD;
> who say to the seers, "See not";
>   and to the prophets, "Prophesy not to us what is right";
> speak to us smooth things,
>   prophesy illusions,
> leave the way, turn aside from the path,
>   let us hear no more of the Holy One of Israel.
>   (Isa. 30:8-11)

The efforts to silence the true prophet are bound to produce louder and more piercing cries (cf. Amos 7:16-17).

The false prophets try to give peace of mind to the powerful with arguments based on their belief that fidelity to the temple cult and worship is a guarantee of political and social security; such arguments are common on the lips of persons who have no real faith nor fear of the LORD. Some of the powerful are godless persons who act as if God did not exist or does not care for earthly problems, since he does not seem to intervene. Micah confronts self-righteous powerful people who have the blessings of the religious establishment; they have no consciousness of doing wrong. They have effectively tamed God at the service of their corruption. They believe that the goodness and patience of God are limitless; and echoing the story of

Balaam (cf. Num. 22–24) they feel that God cannot have Jacob cursed, since God is unconditionally on Jacob's side and the LORD's promises are good forever. They know the works of God in favor of his people; his strong arm saved the people from Egypt, and is still strong enough to save from any adverse circumstances. The Spirit of the LORD does not fail; as in the days of the Judges, the Spirit of God is a mighty savior coming to rescue his people, because he is slow to anger and always ready to forgive. The false prophets are overconfident because they think that they know God's ways so well and that he is forever unconditionally on their side (cf. 3:4, 11).

The questions the false prophets ask imply a strong negative answer, for the LORD in no way can fail his people, no matter how many times the people fail him. The false prophets are deluded in their belief that the divine promises are valid for those who willingly continue to disobey him. The patience and saving power of God become the incentive for their perseverance in corruption and exploitation; divine mercy led them to be merciless with the poor. For Micah, as for Paul, the patience and goodness of God is an invitation to repentance (cf. Rom. 2:1-11). God is good towards those who are good (cf. Ps. 18:25-26); the persons Micah had in mind were not good, but thieves, exploiters and oppressors of the poor, birds of prey, as he will specify in Mic. 2:8-10. The adversaries Micah confronted considered themselves to be the cream of the people, the real "people of God," of which the rich and the poor, the oppressors and the oppressed were equally members; but from Micah's perspective the "remnant," the poor and the weak, will be the authentic people of God. Race and external religion are not the criteria that make up the people of God, but the justice and loving compassion of its members. Those who listen and obey the Word of the LORD will be the ones who are truly his people.

Micah attacks the false prophets in much stronger terms than does his contemporary, Isaiah, because he feels more deeply for the people who are oppressed. Some authors are of the opinion that the strong denunciations of Micah are due to the fact that his authority, as in the case of Jeremiah, was more challenged by his enemies.

Micah answers the efforts to silence him with a stronger and more direct accusation, giving the impression that he has in mind horizons beyond the limits of a small country village, and embracing the capital city itself. Micah sees an ongoing class struggle; the powerful and the rich with their allies, the false prophets, have declared war against the peaceful, the poor, and the innocent (cf. Deut. 24:12-13). They are the true and internal enemies of the people of God, much worse than the Assyrians; their main victims are the poor, the widows, and the orphans—the persons who had to be protected most from injustice according to the laws of the Covenant.

The rich whom Micah has in mind here are those merciless creditors who take away the clothing of the poor, casting aside the basic norms of the Covenant (cf. Exod. 22:26-27). They have no consideration for anyone's condition; their experience in extortion has rendered them callous to other people's sentiments. The text of Mic. 2:8 is not clear; it indicates that the first victims of greed are "those who pass by trustingly with no thought of war." Given the textual difficulty, it could refer to exactions from passersby; it could also apply to those refugees from the north who had barely escaped from the ruin of Samaria, only to find predators and slave traders instead of brothers and sisters among the inhabitants of the south (cf. Amos 1:6, 9). Those who had escaped plunder and defeat elsewhere found a worse enemy in Judah; those who came seeking security found themselves more insecure than ever. These oppressors made no distinction of victims; they took advantage of strong men (Mic. 2:8) as well as of the weak and the powerless (v. 9).

Micah returns to the theme of the accusation of vv. 2-3, denouncing the expropriation of the poor. Women (i.e., widows) are expelled from their homes, while their children are deprived of their honor and dignity by being sold into slavery (cf. 2 Kgs. 4:1); the husbands are not mentioned, since probably they have been killed. The LORD had given the Promised Land as a guarantee for the freedom and dignity of all, from generation to generation, but the rich do not care for the designs of the LORD. They "drive out" or evict the poor, with the same cruelty as an enemy at war evicts the inhabitants of a city to drive them out into exile. The oppressors are creating a new class of internal refugees who have no other choice than to become squatters or to sell themselves as slaves.

Micah 2:10 is still more ambiguous than the preceding verse. It is not clear whether these words are used by the creditors as they drive out the poor from their lands and homes, or whether they constitute a fitting judgment of God after the accusations of the preceding verses. It seems better to continue reading them in parallelism with the oracle of vv. 3-5; Micah continues his threat of dispossession of the rich and the powerful. Before he had threatened them with not participating in the future distribution of the land; now the threat is the added calamity of exile. The rich will be driven out and will have no rights to the land, to the place of rest for God's people (cf. Num. 10:33; Deut. 12:9; Ps. 95:11). The punishment is deserved because of their "uncleanness" with which they have defiled the land; their impurity is not due to sexual deviations or to the adoration of other gods, but to the social injustices they commit. More than other crimes, social injustice defiles the land, fills it with violence, and calls for exemplary punishments from God (cf. Gen. 6:11-13; Lev. 18:25-28; Hos. 4:1-3; Amos 3:9-12).

The rich and the powerful get the punishment that fits them best. They like inanities and empty words, so they will get them. Since they are false listeners who like to listen only to that which pleases them, they will be punished with false prophets, without inspiration or sincerity (cf. 1 Kgs. 22:5-29); these will not give them the Word of God, but they will substitute denunciations for a toast and calls to penance for invitations to banquets; those who love wine in excess deserve a prophet who is a drunk, one who appeals to their lower instincts or one who promises only material rewards. The rich and the powerful are so engrossed in their material pursuits that they do not really care for God nor neighbor; they are outside the realm of the Covenant. With their values and attitudes, "this people" cannot be looked upon by Yahweh as "my people." By preferring the spirit of the false prophets to the true prophets of Yahweh, the powerful are guilty of blasphemy against the Spirit of Yahweh and are beyond salvation (cf. Mark 3:28-30).

The concluding section of this oracle (Mic. 2:12-13) is a classic promise of salvation. It points to the hand of a later editor, alternating oracles of doom with oracles of hope. Some authors see in these verses the response of the false prophets to the verdict just announced by Micah; the following verse (3:1) also begins with a clearly contrasting prophetic message, "But I said," that seems to indicate that the present oracle came from the mouth of the adversaries. The false prophets, instead of ruin and exile, announce security and permanence in the land for the rich.

The image of God as shepherd leading his flock also appears in 4:6-7; the two texts are similar in content and vocabulary and point to the same hand, whether editorial or prophetic; some authors transfer 2:12-13 after 4:7 to create a more harmonious reading, but the text as it stands makes perfect sense. The editor of

Micah has put this oracle of salvation in the mouth of the false prophets who prevent the conversion of the powerful by means of their false promises and assurances of salvation, celebration, and political glory. The words of the false prophets would be perfectly true, but only outside a context of social injustice.

The scattered people of Israel and Judah will be gathered together by God, who is the shepherd of his people (cf. Ps. 23). The last word of God is not to be punishment and exile (Mic. 2:10), but salvation, at least for some. There will be a "remnant" with which the LORD will make a new beginning. This promise had a deeper meaning for the Jews returning from the Babylonian exile when, few in numbers, they missed the old noisy multitudes at the feasts and the pomp of royal celebrations.

The prophet—editor or false prophets—seems to be thinking of a new Exodus and Conquest. God will go before his people as he did in the days of Moses, and will open a breach as in the old days at Jericho (cf. Ps. 68:2-3; Num. 10:35; Josh. 6:20-21). Micah 2:13 is possibly an allusion to a yearly celebration of the conquering power of the LORD, with a solemn procession around the walls of Jerusalem, a ritual associated with the memory of the conquest of Jericho (cf. Josh. 6:1-20; Isa. 26:1), and well expressed in the words of the psalmist:

Walk about Zion, go round about her,
    number her towers,
consider well her ramparts,
    go through her citadels;
that you may tell the next generation
    that this is God,
our God for ever and ever.
    He will be our guide for ever. (Ps. 48:12-14)

Verses 5-6 of this psalm are often seen as an allusion to the Syro-Ephraimite war and to the invasion of Sennacherib, both from Micah's time, although the psalm might have been written at a later date, in the time of Nehemiah (cf. Jerusalem Bible notes).

DENUNCIATIONS AGAINST THE AUTHORITIES (3:1-4)

As in the preceding chapter of Micah, we find again three oracles of similar length, with the middle one dealing with the false prophets (Mic. 3:5-8). There is also a marked parallelism between the first and the third oracles (vv. 1-4 and vv. 9-12). As we mentioned above, the opening words of this oracle set it in contrast with the preceding one from the mouth of the false prophets.

The prophet speaks to the "heads of Jacob and rulers of the house of Israel" (v. 1), not in a geographical and political but in a theological sense. He does not speak to the people of the north but to his own people, those military officers and royal officials who came from Jerusalem to the fortresses around Moresheth; those responsible for the administration of justice are guilty of the serious injustices that are taking place. When injustice takes hold of the very tribunals and persons that are meant to give justice, the situation is almost hopeless. Amos, when confronted with a similar situation, considered it useless to keep on speaking:

> Therefore he who is prudent will keep silent in such a time;
> for it is an evil time. (Amos 5:13)

Micah, on the other hand, brings his denunciations to a maximum, and concludes with the unprecedented threat of the destruction of the city and its temple (Mic. 3:9-12).

Micah attacks those who are supposed to know the Law but who violate it openly (v. 1). Those who must take an interest in the plight of the poor and listen to their cries because it is their job, but who disregard righteousness and turn their backs on them, are the ones most guilty of antisocial conduct. They render no service while they serve themselves at the expense of the poor. Some authors are of the opinion that Micah's denunciations do not include the king directly, because farmers and poor people did not put the blame on the "sacred" king but on his bad counselors and court officials. The king, at least in Judah, enjoyed more respect because of his connection with David. Isaiah is a great apologist for the Davidic line. But, as we said above, for Micah nothing sinful is untouchable, not even the holy city and the temple, and much less a king who could easily be replaced by a successor.

The leaders "hate the good and love the evil" (v. 2); they have a passion for injustice, just as the true prophet has a passion for justice. As in 2:2, Micah speaks of the internal attitudes of the leaders, for they are at the root of the evils that afflict the land. Micah uses the proverbial expressions "hate" and "love" in the most proper and emphatic sense. These words, good and evil, embrace the whole realm of justice and injustice in human dealings. Contemporary prophets spoke in similar terms:

> Seek good, and not evil,
>   that you may live;
> and so that the LORD, the God of hosts, will be with you,
>   as you have said.
> Hate evil, and love good,
>   and establish justice in the gate;
> it may be that the LORD, the God of hosts,
>   will be gracious to the remnant of Joseph.
>   (Amos 5:14-15; cf. also Isa. 1:16-17; 5:20)

The leaders are totally perverted, and so only lawlessness and heartless cruelty can be expected from them. Amos speaks of their banquets with choice foods and wines as well as their music; the psalms and proverbs speak of the rich who devour the people of the LORD (cf. Ps. 14:4; Prov. 30:14). Micah resorts to extremely crude and violent language. The leaders who wantonly ignore justice are inhuman butchers and cannibals; instead of shepherds, they are wolves who tear their victims apart (cf. Zeph. 3:3; Ezek. 34:2-3). They are worse than a plague or a war, enemies of the people and sources of violence.

The accusation of Micah is intense and passionate; he repeats and stresses his ideas without a clear order. He climaxes the accusation with the words:

> [They] break their bones in pieces,
>   and chop them up like meat in a kettle,
> like flesh in a caldron. (Mic. 3:3)

These words recall similar expressions found in 1 Sam. 2:14, indicating that the service of injustice also has a religious character. They, furthermore, alternate their injustices with the empty practices of ritualistic piety.

The verdict, after the accusation, anticipates the divine judgment which will not fail (Mic. 3:4). Since these sinners do not listen to the LORD, the LORD will not listen to them, for God closes himself to those who close themselves to the needs of others (cf. Job 13:22). Their punishment exemplifies the saying of Proverbs:

> He who closes his ear to the cry of the poor
>   will himself cry out and not be heard. (Prov. 21:13)

The oppressors, whose real god is Mammon, will find out that the LORD has closed his ears to them because their religion has nothing in common with the true God (cf. Amos 5:21-24).

The punishment does not sound severe at first, unless we have in mind that "crying" to the LORD is an expression used in Scripture for situations of harsh oppression and disgrace (cf. Exod. 2:23-24; 3:7; Judg. 3:9-15; 6:6-7; 1 Sam. 7:8-9; etc.). They will "cry" to the LORD when the hour of punishment comes, when they will lose their lands and go into exile (cf. Mic. 2:3-5, 10). The punishment is similar to that of Amos 8:11-12, when they will experience the loss and absence of God, a true hell. God listens to those who cry to him, but the oppressors do not realize that there is a time for mercy and a time for judgment. Conversion must take place here and now, and later it will be impossible or useless.

God "will hide his face from them" and will not show mercy to them nor bless them (cf. Isa. 1:15; 8:17; Deut. 31:17-18). They will be desolate. Their situation will be the opposite of what is envisioned in the Priestly blessing, where the LORD is asked to make his face shine upon his people with protection, gracious blessing, and peace (cf. Num. 6:24-26).

ACCUSATION AGAINST THE FALSE PROPHETS (3:5-8)

Prophet Micah again takes issue with the false prophets who lead the people astray; they support the powerful and keep them deceived with a false peace of mind. In this section we find again a messenger formula followed by both a generic and a specific accusation (Mic. 3:5) with the corresponding punishments (vv. 6-7); Micah concludes, by way of contrast, with a description of the activity and mission of the true prophet of the LORD.

The false prophets had made an alliance with the rich to be able to share in the spoils of the poor. They announced a false peace to the oppressors against whom they should have declared a holy war. The false prophets were aware of the commandments of God and of the demands of justice, but the money of the rich proved to be too strong a temptation for them. They had set their eyes on money rather than on God. They had developed what J. L. Sicre calls "a theology of oppression" which seeks to rationalize injustice with religious arguments, false oracles, and visions, which serve to calm the conscience of the oppressors who thus can enjoy their wealth without scruples.

The false prophets were not guided by the Spirit of God; it was the spirit of self-interest and the gifts they received that determined the nature and content of their message. Although it was normal and accepted practice that prophets be paid for their services (cf. 1 Sam. 9:8; 1 Kgs. 14:3; 2 Kgs. 4:42; Amos 7:12-13), in Micah's time the message had been accommodated to the pocket of the person asking for advice. The rich were thus blessed with a false and superficial peace, considering themselves pious and generous because they supported the prophets who claimed to be men of God; the support was mutual and not disinterested. The poor, victimized from all directions, did not receive attention and heard only critcisms and complaints, for the false prophets had declared an open war against them. Micah's denunciation of a false and superficial peace was taken up again and proclaimed by later prophets (cf. Jer. 6:14; Ezek. 13:10; Lam. 2:14).

The true prophet was to be concerned with the principles of justice, of good and evil, which were to give true peace, inner strength, and consistency to the social structures. The adversaries, the false prophets, thought more in terms of politics and exterior peace as well as of the advantages they could derive from the internal social situation. Some think that Micah did not see himself as a prophet but as a defender of the poor; but since the false prophets pretended to speak in the name of God, it was necessary to affirm that he had received the Spirit and the Word of the LORD (cf. Mic. 3:8).

The punishment announced will fit the crime (v. 6). Since the true God is outside their plans and desires, and since they take no direction from his commands, God will render them incapable of receiving his message. Since they have put to a bad use the gifts of God, they will be deprived of them; they will have neither vision nor visions, and their clients will abandon them. They will be disqualified and debarred, becoming obscure and forgotten. The silence of God will reduce them to silence. They will not even be able to know how to deceive and continue their trade. They will be truly dumb.

The shame and sorrow of the false prophets will be public. Their predictions of peace will be proven false, for the most terrible fortunes of war will fall upon them when Jerusalem and the temple are destroyed. Those who once listened to the false prophets will be the first to reject and condemn them. "They shall all cover their lips" (v. 7), or their moustache, as an expression of wonder and amazement at the action of God or because they will have nothing to say. They will cover their faces with sorrow to hide their shame when their divorce from God becomes open knowledge (cf. Lev. 13:45; Ezek. 24:17, 22).

Micah declares himself led by the Spirit of God, that force which in the Old and New Testaments is often associated with struggle against the enemies of God and the establishment of equity and justice. Because he possesses the Spirit, the true prophet becomes a fighter. In Scripture all the battles for the kingdom of God are inspired by his Spirit: It moves the judges to confront the enemies of Israel (cf. Judg. 3:10; 11:29; 14:6, 19). It can help elders to administer justice by avoiding discrimination (cf. Num. 11:16-17; Deut. 1:16-18); it moves the prophets in their relentless striving for justice (cf. Isa. 11:2; 42:1; 61:1-2). In the NT it is also the Spirit that will come to the rescue of the disciples as they fight for their lives before the world's tribunals of justice (cf. Matt. 10:19-20); the Spirit strengthens the community and enables Christians to confront the world and its sin and injustice (cf. John 14:16-18; 16:7-11). It was only on Pentecost, when the Christian community was filled with the Spirit, that there was perfect sharing and equality, oneness without division, one heart and one mind. But that ideal situation did not last long, so the apostles had to appoint seven deacons—men filled with the Spirit—so that they would administer justice and prevent discrimination. It is, finally, the Spirit that made the apostolic Church open its doors to the Gentiles and put an end to religious and racial discrimination (cf. Acts 10:44-48; 11:12-18).

The true prophet is filled with power, spirit, justice, and might (Mic. 3:8); these terms seem to be almost synonymous. The prophet is a fighter like the Man of La Mancha, a Quixote, who dares to fight for an impossible dream of justice; he is bold and daring, exposing injustices and transgression, for he has faith that good will eventually triumph. The prophet is a lone warrior, sometimes feeling isolated, although he is close to the people because he has at heart the interests of the real people, the poor. These are the people the authorities were supposed to defend, but upon whom they actually trample (cf. vv. 1, 9).

ACCUSATION AGAINST JUDGES, PRIESTS, AND PROPHETS (3:9-11)

Micah meets head-on the ruling classes of Jerusalem, and in particular those persons who by reason of their function were seen as especially close to God. Priests and prophets were obviously linked with God, and in a particular way the judges were God's agents, since judgment belonged to the LORD (cf. Mic. 7:9; Deut. 1:17; 32:41; Hos. 5:1; 6:5); judges administered justice in accordance with God's law and were guided by his Spirit (cf. Num. 11:16-30; Isa. 4:4; 28:6). Micah announces that the failure to discharge properly "religious" duties will lead to the destruction of the religious establishment centered around the temple (Mic. 3:12).

The accusations against "religious" leaders mark the climax of Micah's prophetic indictment. He goes to the root of the evil, their internal disposition: "who abhor justice and pervert all equity" (v. 9). They are in direct opposition to God, who abhors injustice and loves justice and equity (cf. Prov. 11:1; 15:9; 17:15; 20:10, 23; Deut. 25:16). These leaders have an instinctive dislike for justice, for they sense that it would question and hinder their enjoyment of the plunder of the poor. Public life was generally marked by corruption and lack of concern for the poor; when it came to corruption and abuse of power, all leaders were equal. The crimes are outlined: they pervert justice and build Zion with blood; greediness rules their lives, and they think that God is unconditionally on their side.

The rulers "build Zion with blood" (Mic. 3:10), in Micah's nerve-shattering imagery. The blood of the poor is converted into money and buildings. Where others see beautiful palaces, comfortable homes, and monumental structures, the prophet sees the human price tag of such apparent prosperity. The riches of the few are based on the poverty of the many. The whole city is but a glittering monument to Mammon. Micah, like Jesus contemplating Jerusalem (cf. Mark 13:1-2), has an "X-ray vision" that penetrates below the surface. Micah and Jesus do not seem to appreciate architectural and artistic values when higher issues are involved. Justice and virtue are the main criteria by which to judge the beauty and stability of a civilization and of the true foundations of social order; without them, the social edifice will collapse with the first storm. The vision of Micah of the bloody city finds a close parallel in Jeremiah's denunciation against King Jehoahaz:

> "Woe to him who builds his house by unrighteousness,
>   and his upper rooms by injustice;
> who makes his neighbor serve him for nothing,
>   and does not give him his wages;
> who says, 'I will build myself a great house

> with spacious upper rooms,'
and cuts out windows for it,
>> paneling it with cedar,
>> and painting it with vermilion.
> Do you think you are a king
>> because you compete in cedar?
> Did not your father eat and drink
>> and do justice and righteousness?
>> Then it was well with him.
> He judged the cause of the poor and needy;
>> then it was well.
> Is not this to know me?
>> says the LORD.
> But you have eyes and heart
>> only for your dishonest gain,
> for shedding innocent blood,
>> and for practicing oppression and violence." (Jer. 22:13-17)

These false leaders, through their unjust sentences, false teachings, and invented oracles, had perverted the social order and had become pillars of injustice and inequity, doomed to failure and ruin.

Micah attacked judges, priests, and prophets more personally because they were the persons to whom the poor could go for help and redress of injustice. God and his justice ought to be their highest priority, but in reality they had all become idolaters whose real god was money. Everything and everyone had a price; services were either for rent or for sale. Judges accepted bribes, and this was a direct violation of the code of the Covenant (cf. Exod. 23:8; Deut. 16:19-20). Priests who were to instruct the people on the rules of community life did so only when induced by money (cf. Exod. 22:9; Deut. 17:8-13; Jer. 18:18; Ezek. 7:26; Hag. 2:11-14). Prophets, as Micah stated before (Mic. 3:5), gave concrete advice but tailored their decisions in accordance with the payments they received.

Although God had little influence in the lives and behavior of the rulers, they "leaned upon the LORD" (v. 11), and felt secure and confident. They were convinced that God was on their side, approving or at least condoning their unjust and criminal practices, values, and interests (cf. Amos 5:14). They often boasted of their relationship with God and professed their faith in him (cf. Mic. 2:7; 3:4-5, 11). They were not very different from those Jeremiah condemned because of their false reliance on the temple of the LORD (cf. Jer. 7:1-4); they were like those about whom Jesus said that they will not enter the kingdom of God, even if they have cried often, "LORD, LORD" (cf. Matt. 7:21). The chosen city of Jerusalem and the temple of Solomon were firm sources of confidence that led to perseverance in the self-satisfied exploitation of others. They did not realize that the presence of God is not incompatible with misfortunes and adversity (Mic. 3:11), but is incompatible with injustice and oppression. God must not become the opium of "pious" evildoers.

THE FINAL SENTENCE:
THE DOOM OF JERUSALEM (3:12)

"The sins of rulers are visited on the heads of their subjects," an old proverb states (cf. 2 Sam. 24). "Because of you," Micah says, the unthinkable is bound to happen. If there are sacred times, places, and objects, for God there is still something more sacred, namely justice and the cry of the poor. A temple can be looked upon by God as no better than a den of thieves (cf. Jer. 7:11; Mark 11:17). Abraham J. Heschel *(The Prophets)* remarks that it would seem incongruous and absurd that because of some minor act of injustice inflicted on the insignificant, powerless poor, the glorious city of Jerusalem should be destroyed and the whole nation go into exile; but the prophets of God are so sensitive to evil that no act of injustice is minor and no person is insignificant or powerless, especially when that person is precious in the eyes of the LORD. God loves justice and the poor more than he loves the temple.

That which the ruling classes of Jerusalem are building with injustice and blood will be torn down by God. Ruin and total desolation will be the result. "Zion shall be plowed as a field," the enemies will not leave one stone upon another (cf. Luke 19:44), and even its foundations will be taken away. As Samaria was to return to its first condition as a vineyard (cf. Mic. 1:6), so Jerusalem will return to nothingness. The temple where the true God has been ignored and insulted will become similar to the high places of the idols which Micah had condemned at the beginning of his work (cf. 1:5). The final sentence of death has been passed.

The words of Micah must have sounded little less than sacrilegious, but they produced a moral impact never envisioned, leading to their first and intended fulfillment, the conversion of the king and the people. The threat was strong enough to strike fear into the hearts of evildoers. One hundred years later, in Jeremiah's time (cf. Jer. 26:17-19), the words of Micah were still remembered. Jesus met with a similar reaction to that of Jeremiah when he spoke of the destruction of the temple, but there was no conversion of the people as there had been in the time of Micah (cf. John 2:18-22; Matt. 26:60-61). The city was not destroyed by the attacking forces of Sennacherib, but the words of Micah acquired particular importance and relevance when history repeated itself and brought the approaching danger of a Babylonian attack. On this occasion, since the prophecy did not produce the desired fruit of conversion, it was fulfilled by God with the destruction of the city and the temple. The book of Lamentations graphically describes this fulfillment of Micah's words:

> For this our heart has become sick,
> for these things our eyes have grown dim,
> for Mount Zion which lies desolate;
> jackals prowl over it. (Lam. 5:17-18)

This section ends with the future of Zion, which will be the subject of the following section. But punishment will not be the final word, for it will be followed by salvation. As Micah stated at the beginning of the section (cf. Mic. 2:1-5), there will be a future distribution of the land and the creation of a new community from which the oppressors and exploiters will be excluded.

The punishment stage will be a tragic purification, after which there will be a spiritual resurrection of a new Jerusalem to be described in the following chapters.

RESTORATION AND SALVATION: THE GREAT DIALOGUE

Micah 4:1–5:15

The oracles of Mic. 4–5 are particularly difficult to interpret because of their striking diversity and contradictory formulations. Scholars are in open disagreement when attempting to solve this puzzle of oracles without apparent solution.

Some authors see this section as a collection of diverse oracles, all dealing with the restoration of Jerusalem and Judah; these are presumed to come from different periods and to have been put together by an editor who wanted to create an atmosphere of hope and optimism after the dire predictions of 3:9-12. The death sentence just pronounced had to be followed by the hope of divine restoration and mercy.

James L. Mays notes the affinity of this section with oracles of Jeremiah and the exilic period (*Micah*, 24ff.). Bruce Vawter accepts a core oracle from the 8th cent. B.C., while attributing the rest to postexilic times (*Amos, Hosea, Micah,* 148). Hans Walter Wolff sees in this section a long redactional unit, based on the original saying of Mic. 3:9-12 (*Micah the Prophet,* 85); this unit is composed of two "then sayings" (4:1-7), a nucleus of "now oracles" (4:8–5:4), and another set of "then sayings" (5:5-15). The "now oracles," dating from the period of the Babylonian crisis, describe the suffering and humiliation of Jerusalem; the "then sayings," from postexilic times, envision the future restoration of Zion and the judgment of the nations. The redactor effectively puts forward a people without a present, dreaming of a rich and glorious future.

Luis Alonso-Schökel, with J. L. Sicre as well as A. S. van der Woude and some others, sees in this section a long dialogue or dispute between Micah or his disciples and the false prophets or those who dream of militarism as the road to liberation and glory. This dialogue is similar to the one insinuated in the preceding section (2:1–3:12). The present form, he declares, has been given a postexilic editor closely associated with the temple and the liturgical life of Judah.

The hypothesis of a dialogue between Micah (or his disciples) and his enemies, the false prophets, seems to be the most coherent and simple suggestion. It explains the content as well as the position of the oracles of this section much better than any theory of later composition, in which varied oracles are said to be brought together whose only link to each other is the general liturgical setting. The dialogue is vivid and aggressive, with one side often echoing words of the other to give them a new twist and meaning.

The principal argument of the dialogue is the when and the how of the coming restoration and salvation. It will not be immediate; it comes after a long period of purification, through suffering and defeat. The city that now oppresses the poor will become someday the liberator of nations. The greatness of Jerusalem will come through a little and humble remnant left from the coming destruction. Salvation will not be obtained by means of the power of arms or idols but solely through the power of God. The glory of Jerusalem will not originate from Jerusalem itself but, as in the days of old, from little Bethlehem, the birthplace of the Davidic dynasty.

The dialogue is marked by clear contrasts and the contradictory opinions of the two sides in dispute. Micah says that many nations shall come to the LORD (4:2), while his adversaries insist that Judah alone will walk in the name of the LORD (v. 5). They say that Zion should not cry aloud like a woman in travail (v. 9), while Micah stresses that Zion should indeed so writhe and groan (v. 10). While the true prophet underscores that the ruler will act only with the power and strength of the LORD (5:4), the false prophets insist on a ruler with a drawn sword (v. 6). The remnant among the nations is seen by Micah as a soft and quiet dew from the LORD (v. 7), while the militarists see the remnant as a rampaging lion among the beasts of the forests (v. 8).

This complicated section can be best understood as a vivid dialogue; the partial transcription that follows will help the reader to better understand the depth of the prophetic message:

Micah:

It shall come to pass in the latter days
    that the mountain of the house of the LORD
shall be established as the highest of the mountains,

43

> and shall be raised up above all the hills;
> and [all the] peoples shall flow to it,
> and many nations shall come. . . . (4:1-2a)

False prophets: (Jerusalem deserves glory but we do not accept the conversion of gentile nations.)

> For all the peoples walk
> each in the name of its god,
> but we will walk in the name of the LORD our God
> for ever and ever. (4:5)

Micah: (The restoration and final glory will start with humble and painful beginnings; the punishment of the present injustices will surely come.)

> In that day, says the LORD,
> I will assemble the lame
> and gather those that have been driven away,
> and those whom I have afflicted;
> and the lame I will make the remnant;
> and those who were cast off, a strong nation;
> and the LORD will reign over them in Mount Zion
> from this time forth and for evermore. (4:6-7)

False Prophets: (You must not speak of affliction and disgrace; the people have nothing to fear.)

> And you, O tower of the flock,
> hill of the daughter of Zion,
> to you shall it come,
> . . . the kingdom of the daughter of Jerusalem.
> Now why do you cry aloud?
> Is there no king in you?
> Has your counselor perished,
> that pangs have seized you like a woman in travail? (4:8-9)

Micah: (The image of a woman in travail you have used is good to describe the punishment that will surely come. The sufferings will lead to a new birth for Zion.)

> Writhe and groan, O daughter of Zion,
> like a woman in travail;
> for now you shall go forth from the city
> and dwell in the open country;
> you shall go to Babylon.

There you shall be rescued,
   there the LORD will redeem you
   from the hand of your enemies. (4:10)

False Prophets: (What Micah is announcing cannot happen since
God is with us, on our side.)

Now many nations
   are assembled against you,
saying, "Let her be profaned,
   and let our eyes gaze upon Zion."
But they do not know
   the thoughts of the LORD,
they do not understand his plan,
   that he has gathered them as sheaves for the threshing floor.
Arise and thresh,
   O daughter of Zion,
for I will make your horn iron
   and your hoofs bronze;
you shall beat in pieces many peoples,
   and shall devote their gain to the LORD,
   their wealth to the LORD of the whole earth. (4:11-13)

Micah: (Punishment is surely coming; salvation will come again,
as in the days of old, from little Bethlehem; from there a shepherd
will come forth.)

Now you are walled about with a wall;
   siege is laid against us;
with a rod they strike upon the cheek
   the ruler of Israel.
But you, O Bethlehem Ephrathah,
   who are little to be among the clans of Judah,
from you shall come forth for me
   one who is to be ruler in Israel . . .
And this shall be peace. (5:1-2, 5a)

False Prophets: (Salvation will be something more spectacular
than that!)

When the Assyrian comes into our land
   and treads upon our soil,
. . . we will raise against him seven shepherds
   and eight princes of men;
they shall rule the land of Assyria with the sword,

and the land of Nimrod with the drawn sword;
and they shall deliver us from the Assyrian
   when he comes into our land
   and treads within our border. (5:5b-6)

Micah: (Salvation will be quiet but effective.)

Then the remnant of Jacob shall be
   in the midst of many peoples
like dew from the LORD,
   like showers upon the grass,
which tarry not for men
   nor wait for the sons of men. (5:7)

False Prophets: (Salvation will not be quiet like the dew but spectacular with military victories.)

And the remnant of Jacob shall be among the nations,
   in the midst of many peoples,
like a lion among the beasts of the forest,
   like a young lion among the flocks of sheep, . . .
Your hand shall be lifted up over your adversaries,
   and all your enemies shall be cut off. (5:8-9)

Micah: (Salvation will come not through the removal of your external enemies, but through the removal of the military strength and the religious idols in which you put your trust.)

And in that day, says the LORD,
   I will cut off your horses from among you
   and will destroy your chariots; . . .
and I will cut off sorceries from your hand,
   and you shall have no more soothsayers;
and I will cut off your images
   and your pillars from among you . . . (5:10-13a)

THE FUTURE RESTORATION OF ZION (4:1-5)

The first three verses of this oracle are also found in Isa. 2:2-4. They announce that the eschatological future of Zion was to be fulfilled only in the messianic era.

Most commentators attribute this oracle to Isaiah, who also in ch. 60 describes the pilgrimage of the converted pagans to Zion. Delbert R. Hillers (*Micah*, 52-53) attributes it to Micah, since the vocabulary is similar to the rest of the book and it is intimately linked to that of the preceding oracle (Mic. 3:9-12). Bruce Vawter thinks that these verses were "common property," without copyright, used by different authors (*Amos, Hosea, Micah,* 149); they were in line with preexilic psalms (cf. Pss. 2, 72) and with the traditional hopes of the triumph of the LORD and the glory of Zion. If Isaiah and Micah did not take the oracle from each other, they could have taken it from an earlier anonymous author or a postexilic redactor may have inserted it in both prophets. In the present setting the vocabulary and contents fit Micah better.

The oracle marks a clear contrast with what precedes. The old plundered and ruined mountain will become a glorious sight; the destroyed temple will become a center of attraction for the whole world; the city of crime and injustice will become the center and focus from which justice will flow into the world. All roads will lead to Jerusalem.

The oracle breathes religious fervor and optimism. The idyllic peace that is to come will be anti-Babel (cf. Gen. 11:8-9) and a great feast of Pentecost (cf. Acts 2:5). A new era will be inaugurated for humanity.

Zion will be exalted and will become the center of a double stream: a stream of pilgrim peoples from all nations will come to Zion, while another stream, that of justice and knowledge of the LORD, will flow out from it. The result will be a reign of universal peace in the world (cf. Ezek. 47:1-12; Joel 3:18; Zech. 14:8).

4:1-2 The restoration of Zion will take place "in the latter days," in an indeterminate future time in which the final era will be installed. After the incredible destruction of the temple and the city, an unbelievable future will follow. The people who seem to have little to look for in the present are promised a future of justice, peace, and prosperity.

Zion shall be established as the highest of the mountains of the world. Canaanite gods were adored on the hills and the high places, but when the time comes the universal sovereignty of God will be recognized by all peoples; they will repeat the traditional liturgical invitation to pilgrimage, "Come, let us go to the mountain of the house of the LORD" (cf. Ps. 122:1, 4); they will come as pilgrims, attracted by the power of the LORD, and not as tourists impressed by the political power of Zion nor by the solemnity of its religious rites.

All the nations will come to the LORD, and Jerusalem will become the ideal messianic city of justice and knowledge of the LORD. The power of money and injustice will be replaced by a divine kingdom. The center of oppression of the poor and the weak will become the center of liberation for all nations. This will happen solely through a divine intervention, for the LORD cannot fail Jerusalem even if the city fails in its fidelity to the LORD.

The nations will form a stream of peoples, becoming a new river bringing joy to the city of God (cf. Pss. 46, 67, 86). They will go to the temple where the priests will give advice and judgment in the name of the LORD. This was not happening during Micah's time, but it always remained as a hope. The nations are to be attracted by the "torah" of the LORD; they will come as disciples to receive instruction on the laws, norms, customs, and traditions of Zion so that they can integrate them into their lives. The result will be a deep change and conversion; they will abandon their idols and will adhere to the ways of the LORD, accepting God's rule and kingdom over them, and producing fruits of peace and justice. Human egotism will be eliminated so there will be no room for fears, hatred, vengeance, or arms.

3-4 The will of God will be the deciding factor in human relations; because of this, v. 3 is seen as a suitable motto for the United Nations. Nations will give peace a chance. Peace followed by arms control or disarmament has never worked in the past, but disarmament will be a necessary step toward authentic peace (cf. Mic. 7:16-17). Peace is inevitable, because that is the will of God. God will eliminate the arms of Israel and Judah as well as those of the world. Nations will put away the psychology of war—*si vis pacem para bellum* ("if you want peace, prepare for war")—and they will do away with armaments needed for conquest and for protection against an unjust setup. The desire for war can and will be conquered by a deeper desire for the knowledge and word of the LORD. Armament policies will be replaced by provision for basic agrarian needs.

Micah, who is a consistent antimilitarist, dreams of a new world full of social possibilities. Using simple agrarian images, he upholds the priority of a farming economy over a militarism which drained all the human and economic resources of the land. Arms were to be converted into instruments of production, since in

Judah—as in many lands today—one cannot have both. The triumph of the LORD will be the death sentence to the arms race (cf. Ps. 46:9-10; Isa. 11:6-9; Jer. 5:17; Zech. 9:10). Judah—as most nations after it—found it difficult to believe in the unlimited power of the politics of peace. Humanity keeps hoping for the days when military maneuvers will be turned into sports festivals, tanks into tractors, bullets into bread, rifles into spades, missiles into fireworks, and planes into agricultural sprayers. Then there will be true prosperity and harmony on earth.

Micah describes the future peace and prosperity with the images of the vine and the fig tree, proverbially used in Scripture to affirm the security, tranquillity, and prosperity of the people (cf. 1 Kgs. 4:25; 2 Kgs. 18:31; Isa. 36:16; Hos. 2:12; Joel 1:12; 2:22; 3:10; Zech. 3:10). Micah's agricultural description probably points to a return to paradisiacal conditions of which prophets often thought (cf. Isa. 65:20-25; Ezek. 36:25; Hos. 2:18).

The vine and the fig tree probably stand for the two main trees of paradise, symbolizing life-joy and knowledge of the LORD (cf. John 1:47-51). The people of Israel, and Christians later, always dreamed of a return to paradise with personal prosperity and security, without danger from wild animals, and with time for the study of the Word of the LORD. Walter Brueggemann sees the vine and the fig tree as simple and modest dreams of farmers, not the dreams of kings and militarists ("Vine and Fig Tree," *Catholic Biblical Quarterly* 43 [1981]: 199). This verse could be in contrast with the glorious eschatological image of the preceding verses. The climax of Mic. 4:4 is the promise of peace, without threats of war or of becoming pawns of war. The final words, "The mouth of the LORD of hosts has spoken," can be read as an emphatic affirmation of the preceding oracle or as a faith response of the community.

5 This verse most probably states the response of the false prophets to the prediction of Micah. When not understood as part of a dialogue, it becomes a puzzling verse (Vawter, 150), or is seen as a gloss that was incorporated into the text, or is considered a later liturgical addition (Jerusalem Bible). The contents of the verse are difficult to reconcile with 4:2, except when seen as a response of Micah's adversaries who reject his universal outlook and insist on their own exclusivist vision of Judah. They do not think of a conversion of pagans or of an integration of nations in the LORD; they affirm their experience of the present and make it final and definitive. They effectively deny Micah's hope for the future.

The enemies of Micah affirm that they will always walk with the LORD, while the prophet has repeatedly denounced them for following their own paths and not the ways of the LORD. "Walk in the name of the LORD"—or "walk with the LORD"—expressed an intimacy with the LORD manifested in loyalty, worship, obedience, social practices, and total reliance on the LORD. Judah, during Micah's time, was walking in the ways of Samaria and of the nations. When Judah will truly walk in the ways of the LORD Micah's vision of an integration of nations will start becoming a reality.

This verse was probably used to call the people of Judah to fidelity during the Exile, and later received an added meaning in a liturgical setting; until today Jews use this verse as an expression of their religious faith as opposed to that of other nations.

New Promise of Restoration (4:6-7)

The true prophet answers with a brief oracle well defined in its beginning and its conclusion. In Mic. 4:1-4 Micah had presented a vision of the "final glory"; now he presents the stages that will lead to that glory. The future kingdom and flock will start from surprisingly humble beginnings.

The promise of restoration is presented under the common scriptural image of a kingdom and a shepherd who rescues and gathers the dispersed flock (cf. Ezek. 34:1-31). It will all come about after a trying and severe punishment. The Exile to which Micah alludes was a cruel reality for the inhabitants of the northern kingdom of Samaria. Even in Judah there had been some territorial losses and partial exiles, so that the worst could be expected to come.

Because of the allusions to the Exile most commentators consider this oracle as a postexilic addition, similar to texts found in Second Isaiah (cf. also Isa. 11:12-16; Zeph. 3:18-20). There is no need to postulate such a late period of composition, although the words of Micah on the destruction of Zion and the return from the Exile must have become particularly meaningful during and after the Babylonian tragedy.

The words of Mic. 4:6, "In that day," refer to a future not as distant as that of vv. 1-4, since the prophet now speaks of the first step in the return from exile; before the stream of nations there will be first a stream of exiles. The survivors of 3:12, depressed and dejected, will experience the unexpected; those who consider themselves as good for nothing will be used by God for the best, to build a new future and inaugurate a glorious era. The remnant, the survivors, will be the witnesses of the action of the LORD and the bearers of the hope of a lasting life blessing by God.

God will build a unique and miraculous kingdom with the poor, the maimed, the blind, and the lame—those on the edge of life (cf. Zeph. 3:12; Isa. 29:18; Luke 14:16-24). The weak who consistently are last will now be first, through the action of the LORD. Dispersion and weakness will be the starting point for God's new plan, putting an end to the old (cf. Mary's Magnificat, Luke 1:46-55).

Historically, this and similar prophecies acquired an added significance at the end of the Babylonian Captivity, but the return of 42,360 Jews from exile and the subsequent restoration did not correspond to the expected glory; the reign of the LORD over Zion forever will be the culmination of history that will make possible the final fulfillment of the prophet's words. Christians see the fulfillment of this and similar prophecies in the new dispensation inaugurated by Jesus of Nazareth.

THE FALSE PROPHETS AND THE GLORIOUS KINGDOM (4:8-9)

The false prophets refuse to face suffering and, rather than expect the worst, like to hope for the best. For them, just because Judah might be under pressure one must not think of destruction and exile. God will surely come to the rescue since his promises to the Davidic dynasty cannot fail.

The "tower of the flock" *(migdal-ʿeder)* of which Micah speaks is probably a fortress within the city of Jerusalem. St. Jerome thinks of a place near Bethlehem (cf. Gen. 35:21); the parallel "*ophel* ('hill') of the daughter of Zion" points to the residence of the royal family. The false prophets probably want to flatter the king. They announce the restoring of the "former dominion," as in the time of David and Solomon when the twelve tribes were united and Israel controlled neighboring lands.

The false prophets want to instill security with a message very different from Micah's. Before, the reason for security was the presence of the temple and the divine promises, while now the royal house seems to be the reason for the confidence of the false prophets. Jerusalem can feel secure as long as the Davidic line rules. Even if the kingdom has been greatly reduced in territory, there still remains the hope for the restoration of the old and glorious empire which will be the earthly and visible expression of the divine rule of the world from Zion, as Micah has just announced.

Mic. 4:9 is seen by many commentators as a later addition announcing the deportation to Babylon. The oracle does have echoes of Jeremiah, and reflects the time of King Zedekiah (ca. 587 B.C.). Some see in it allusions to the period of Zerubbabel (ca. 516), when efforts were made to restore the monarchy. I would prefer to see in it an oracle of Micah which has been adapted later by an editor to the situation of the Babylonian Exile. The city has a call to relive the ancient greatness, so it must not shrink and be afraid because of pressures. The presence of the Davidic king is a firm reason for hope. The present sufferings are just the birth pangs, irresistible, painful, and inevitable, but they open the door to the new era. Confidence through pain and suffering paves the way to salvation. The confidence of Jerusalem is anchored in the LORD who dwells in her midst. Verse 9 could be interpreted in the light of the close parallel of Jer. 8:19:

> Hark, the cry of the daughter of my people
>   from the length and the breadth of the land:
> "Is the LORD not in Zion?
>   Is her King not in her?"
> "Why have they provoked me to anger with their graven
>   images,
>   and with their foreign idols?"

The true king of Zion is the LORD who dwells in her. The false prophets remind the people of the power of the presence of the LORD. Micah would stress that their king is a man, useless for comfort, adding that they have ignored the laws of the LORD, thus effectively negating his power and kingship over them.

SALVATION THROUGH SUFFERING,
NOT THROUGH MILITARY VICTORY (4:10-13)

Micah takes over the vocabulary and imagery of the false prophets and turns it against them. If they say that Zion should not act as a helpless woman in labor, Micah contradicts them, announcing that the worst is yet to come. Zion and Judah will go from bad to worse, from the siege to captivity. Salvation will come at the end. These two oracles (Mic. 4:10 and 11-13) remind us of similar oracles of Isaiah relating to the time of the invasion of Sennacherib. Jerusalem besieged and liberated was a common and typical theme (cf. Isa. 10:24-27, 32-34; 14:24-27; 29:1-8; 30:27-33; 31:4-9). Micah foresees an exile which will end in rescue and liberation. The people of Judah will dwell in the open country, either because their cities have been conquered and destroyed or because the cities have become insecure (cf. Jer. 6:1; 10:17). The vocabulary of this oracle is reminiscent of that of Exodus. The people will be led to the open country, to the desert (as in Hos. 2:14), to a place of conversion through undistracted confrontation with God. "There," in the midst of their misery, they will experience salvation and new life.

The allusion to Babylon is generally seen as a later addition which was introduced by an editor who adapted the original text of Micah of Moresheth to later conditions. Yehezkel Kaufmann is of the opinion that the original text of Micah had in mind the Assyrians, rather than the Babylonians (*The Religion of Israel from Its Beginnings to the Babylonian Exile*, 352).

The false prophets are blind to the reality in which they live. They do not see evil in their society. Rather than think of defeat and exile, they dream of military victories and gain. They daringly claim to know — better than Micah — God's plan for Zion. They lean on the traditional hope of the defeat of the nations, because they believe God cannot fail his city. This text has a close parallel in 1 Kgs. 22:5-25, where false prophets, reflecting a similar attitude, honor horns as a symbol of strength and destruction.

The words of the false prophets in Mic. 4:11-13 are commonly seen as a postexilic addition that might reflect the opposition of the neighboring nations to the restoration of Judah and Jerusalem. It is better to see this passage as coming from Micah's time, in connection with the armies from many nations brought by the Assyrian king Sennacherib against Judah. The false prophets reflect the old hope expressed in Ps. 2: the enemies gather together but are doomed to destruction.

Micah 4:11-12 recalls the rumors of the Assyrian campaigns, which were strong enough to put fear in the hearts of the people. Fear could drive them to conversion, but the false prophets see no need for change since God cannot fail to do his part. The attack and the defeat of many nations later became a favorite theme in eschatology (cf. Ezek. 38–39; Joel 3; Zech. 12:1-9). Zion should resist with confidence, since history is not in the hands of the superpowers but in the hands of God. God's plan is the only one that counts, and he has gathered them as sheaves for the threshing floor, where they will be shredded and totally destroyed (cf. 2 Kgs. 13:7; Isa. 21:10; 41:15; Jer. 51:33; Amos 1:3; Hab. 3:12). The false prophets, developing a theology of oppression, announce an easy hope that does not require any personal conversion nor any change in the unjust social situation.

The false prophets invite Zion to wage a holy war against the nations, consecrating the peoples to religious destruction and annihilation (Mic. 4:13). The false prophets do not look at the future envisioned by Micah in which all the nations will someday be converted to justice and peace and attracted to God in Jerusalem. Zion, like a wild calf, is to destroy with the power and strength of its horns. Thus the false prophets promise more oppressive and destructive power to the very city which has been denounced by Micah as the oppressor of the poor and the weak (3:2-3, 9-12). They are blind to the relationship between justice and peace; they believe that God is unconditionally on their side and that victory will be theirs since God is the LORD of the whole earth (cf. Josh. 3:11, 13; Ps. 65:5; Zech. 4:14; 6:5).

SALVATION THROUGH A RETURN TO THE HUMBLE DAVIDIC BEGINNINGS (5:1-6a)

The answer of Micah to the predictions of the false prophets has a deliberately mysterious tone. Micah uses metaphoric language with references to legends and traditions about which we know very little; thus he sheds light on his thoughts but invites the hearer to look more diligently. He corrects the ideas of the false prophets to prevent false hopes and dreams. He distinguishes a "now," a period of trial, from a distant future when the old glories will rise again. The present situation is a challenge to the faith of the people and to the action of God. Salvation will come once again from David, from little Bethlehem, in the distant future of messianic times.

The text of Mic. 5:1 (4:14 in the Hebrew text) is obscure. It could be read as an invitation to strengthen the walls for resistance or as a statement on the combined attack of the nations. The prophet establishes a contrast between the now humiliated, strongly fortified, and proud city and the humble condition of Ephrathah from which salvation will come. The king, now humiliated and the object of derision, is contrasted with the glorious ruler who is to come forth. The present king, Hezekiah in the time of Sennacherib, is "stricken upon the cheek." The Assyrian king claimed to have shut Hezekiah "like a bird in a cage" during the siege of Jerusalem (cf. 2 Kgs. 18:17-37; Isa. 36:1-22). Though seriously pressed and insulted, the present king derived strength to fight from the divine promise of better times and of a glorious offspring (cf. also Isa. 7:13-16).

Micah 5:2-3 (Hebrew 5:1-2) contains one of the best known "messianic prophecies." The announcement of the promised "Messiah," since the writing of the Gospels, has been consistently interpreted by the Fathers of the Church and by most commentators in reference to Jesus' birth in Bethlehem; they saw the OT in its relationship to the NT. Micah, as his contemporary Isaiah in the Immanuel oracle (cf. Isa. 7:14), probably did not look to a far and distant future but at something relatively near to him. The text is particularly difficult because of the ambiguity that sometimes characterizes prophetic threats and promises. The prophet seems to avoid concrete details of the fulfillment, since he was aware of the certainty of the restoration to come but did not know the exact way in which God was to bring it about. It must be remembered that the prophecies, more than chronological predictions, are often timeless affirmations of a faith and hope of Israel which will eventually be realized in time.

Ephrathah was originally designated a clan, related to Caleb, which was established in the vicinity of Bethlehem of Judah (cf. 1 Chr. 2:19, 24, 50; 1 Sam. 17:12; Ruth 1:2). Another Bethlehem was located in the territory of Zebulun (cf. Josh. 19:15). Etymologically, Ephrathah was "the fruitful one," rich in grain, oil, wine, and figs; now it was going to produce an extraordinary fruit, the savior, the "Messiah."

Micah underscores that Bethlehem was little among the clans (literally, "the thousands") of Judah, using an ancient vocabulary from the period of the Judges. Micah, like most prophets, when announcing the future takes a look at the past. He thinks of the origins of the house of David, looking back three hundred years to a period that was becoming legendary (cf. 1 Sam. 17:12-13; Ruth 4:11, 17, 18-22).

Bethlehem is the reminder of the ancient promises to David and his house which the present sins and injustices of Jerusalem cannot invalidate. Isaiah thought highly of the capital city, while Micah looked for salvation from the countryside. For Micah Jerusalem has shown that it has no future except destruction, because it has become the center of exploitation. The future lies with little and rural Bethlehem, which will again bring forth a leader like David—animated by the same spirit, a source of fresh hope who will do away with decadence, apostasy, and injustice (cf. Neh. 12:46; Amos 9:11). Sometimes, when confronted with a political or social crisis, we—like Micah—look back at our own historical past to dream of leadership for the future; thus, some will say that today's world needs a new Lincoln, a new Gandhi, or a new Kennedy. It is always hoped and desired that the future leadership will avoid the pitfalls, mistakes, and deficiencies of the past.

Micah announces that the leader "shall come forth" from Bethlehem; later tradition and exegesis interpreted this as a reference to the physical birth of the Messiah (cf. Matt. 2:6; John 7:42). Micah repeats here a recurrent theme in the OT: a small place produces a great man, and out of ruins and humiliation comes forth glory. God will again choose Bethlehem and not Zion, the humble and the small to shame the strong and the powerful.

The leader who is to come forth is not called "king" but "ruler," for he shall be the ideal shepherd who will establish the sole kingship of the LORD.

Micah's mysterious language becomes still more difficult in Mic. 5:3. He speaks of the human origin of the future ruler, mentioning only the mother of the one to be born. This emphasis on the role of the woman-mother calls to mind the oracle of Isa. 7:14, given some twenty-five years earlier and with which Micah was probably familiar.

Using the metaphor of a woman's pregnancy, the text could mean that God will abandon his people only for a brief period. Then a new birth of freedom and justice will take place, and the old order and unity will be restored. The announcement of a future glorious ruler does not exclude a period of tribulation and suffering; from the moment the savior is announced history becomes pregnant and groans for the birth of a new age (cf. Rom. 8:18-22).

The expected restoration, as in other prophets, has two themes: women, and one woman in particular, give birth again; and the exiles come back home from the Diaspora (cf. Isa. 7:14; 9:6; 10:21-22; Jer. 31:16, 17, 22). Some authors, basing their opinion on the preceding context of Mic. 4:9, 10, have identified Zion as "she who is in travail"; others have applied it to the Synagogue or to some other woman such as the wife of a king or of a prophet. As in the text of Isa. 7:14, the text here has also been read by Christians in the light of its fulfillment in the NT with reference to Mary, the mother of Jesus.

Micah stresses the Davidic overtones of his prediction, speaking of "his brethren" who will return from captivity. In the same way as David ruled "in the midst of his brothers" (1 Sam. 6:13), the one to be born will bring about unity and national reconciliation, an important theme in oracles of restoration (cf. 2 Sam. 5:1-5; Isa. 11:13; Jer. 33:14; Ezek. 37:15-28).

The future peace is announced in Mic. 5:4-5b. The Messiah, more than a king, will be a "shepherd." Micah affirms the Davidic promise of 2 Sam. 7:9 and asserts that the flock will be gathered by the LORD and entrusted to his Chosen One. "He shall stand," a possible allusion to a royal coronation, with the power and majesty of the LORD his God. His rule and reign will be an expression and a sacrament of the rule and shepherding of the LORD.

The future shepherd will feed his flock, guiding and protecting it, taking care of its needs. The sheep will dwell secure, and there shall be peace in the land. Micah announces in a new form and with a new image the universal peace he had envisioned at the beginning of this section (Mic. 4:1-4), when nations shall renounce military ventures and people will dwell secure under the vine and the fig tree (cf. 4:3-4).

The ideal presented by Micah is similar to that of Isa. 9:5, and to that which is repeatedly expressed in Ps. 72:

> Give the king thy justice, O God,
>   and thy righteousness to the royal son!
> May he judge thy people with righteousness,
>   and thy poor with justice!
> Let the mountains bear prosperity (*shalom*) for the people,
>   and the hills, in righteousness! (Ps. 72:1-3)

Peace is consistently associated with justice to such a degree that peace and justice become almost synonymous terms. Without justice and the protection of the poor, there can be only a false peace such as the one often proclaimed by the false prophets. The true prophet announces a true and lasting peace which, through a personal conversion, heals the wounds of injustice.

The hope heralded in Ps. 72 as well as in Isaiah and Micah was not limited to a single individual, a "messiah" who would come once and for all. At the coronation of a new king, the people affirmed with greater intensity than in the past the hope that the Davidic promise and a kingdom of peace and justice would become a reality. A new king could lead the people to dream of a new era, especially for the disadvantaged and the poor. The promises made to David were to be fulfilled in the same manner as the promises made to Abraham, through a gradual and silent unfolding throughout history.

The flock of the shepherd, echoing King Solomon's reign, will extend "to the ends of the earth," for his rule shall be universal, like that of the LORD. "[He] shall be peace," or "Prince of Peace" in the expression of Isa. 9:5, the author of reconciliation and peace.

PEACE THROUGH THE ACTION OF THE LORD, NOT THROUGH MILITARY VICTORY (5:6b-9)

Micah's ideas about the origin and nature of peace forcefully clash with those of his adversaries. The false prophets propose an idea of peace in harmony with their already expressed military views. They have a false security and dream of a false peace based on the force of arms rather than on social justice and reform; thus they contradict the authentic "messianic" hope for a lasting peace.

The false prophets unveil their imperial dreams just before the invasion of the Assyrian king Sennacherib. They hope that when Assyria attacks, Israel will have a number of allies, "seven or eight," more than sufficient to defeat the enemy. Victory is assured (cf. Mic. 5:5b-6). Assyria is mentioned by name, for in the time of Micah it had become the classical enemy of Judah. Later, Babylon and Edom will become the living symbols of enmity.

The false prophets make a literal rebuttal of the preceding oracle. Micah had announced a deliverer from the LORD, while the false prophets take upon themselves the burden of deliverance;

independently of what the LORD might have in mind as expressed in the words of Micah, they will take the initiative and will raise armed leaders who will protect their own land and borders. Micah had announced *one* deliverer from the LORD; the false prophets announce *seven or eight* saviors. Micah had stated that the savior would proceed "in the strength of the LORD" (v. 4), like David going to battle against Goliath; the false prophets answer back with seven chieftains who will deliver them and will rule *by the power of their swords*. In their view, salvation will come in their own spectacular terms and not as announced by Micah.

Micah answers the false prophets with the announcement that peace and salvation will come, not through military victory but through the silent action of the LORD that will result in the conversion of nations (v. 7). This oracle marks a clear antithesis to the oracles that precede and follow, both characterized by a militaristic perspective. The literary parallelism between this oracle of Micah and the response of his enemies serves to underline the contrast between two hopes.

Micah thinks of the remnant of Jacob as the community of scattered, lame, and afflicted sheep that the LORD will gather in Zion (cf. 4:6-7), the future religious center of the world and the light of the nations (cf. 4:1-4). Israel and Judah will be a source of divine blessings in an unexpected manner. The remnant community will be like a dew, a silent, mysterious, and efficacious gift from God which gives fertility to the fields (cf. Ps. 133:3; Prov. 19:12). Micah offers a humble but optimistic view of the future of Israel which will not ultimately depend on human beings but on the action of God.

The false prophets take Micah's oracle and twist it to express their own view that salvation will come through the destruction of the enemies. They claim that the remnant of Jacob will not be a blessing like the dew but rather a curse like a lion, a source of harm and destruction. The false prophets incite to war as a road to peace, rather than exhort to conversion. The lion is presented as an apt symbol because it is a destroyer, an implacable animal that kills at no risk and does not respect the weakness of the sheep; it was the emblem of the tribe of Judah and of the city of Jerusalem (cf. Num. 23:24; 24:9). The mysterious power of the dew comes from God, while the lion trusts in its own strength.

The oracle concludes in Mic. 5:9 with what can be constructed as a liturgical prayer or as an oracular prediction of the false prophets. Their prayer or announcement stating that the enemies will be "cut off" will be answered by the following oracle, which turns their words against them and their expectations.

SALVATION THROUGH DIVINE PURIFICATION (5:10-15)

Micah has the last word in his protracted argument with the false prophets; he takes their own word "cut off" and turns it against new targets. The sentences of Micah's answer are arranged in strict, repetitious, and cumulative symmetry to announce more graphically the systematic purification that is to come, in order to open the door to an era of peace.

God will cut off and eradicate, not so much the *external enemies* against whom the false prophets raved, but the *internal enemies* of the people, the roots of injustice and the bases for human confidence that excluded God: the military and political power, the instruments of divination and sorcery that call attention away from God, and the idols that directly oppose the rule of the true God (cf. Ps. 20:7; Isa. 2:6-8). The people had proven incapable of purifying themselves; the reform of King Hezekiah had fallen short. God himself would have to purify his people to prepare the land for the rule of the messianic king who would bring true peace and justice to the land, setting as the foundation of his reign the defense of the rights of the poor.

The great purification by God will not be simply a punishment but a final salvific act. God will take away human securities so that the people will trust in him alone and will heed his call to conversion and justice.

Horses and chariots will be eliminated so that there will be a real chance for peace (cf. Mic. 4:3-4). When God will reign in the world, military armaments and fortifications will become superfluous and obsolete as a source of protection, trust, or pride (cf. Hos. 14:3; Isa. 31:1). As Amos places idols and ostentatious riches on equal footing before God (cf. Amos 3:14-15; 5:25-26), so Micah views armaments and idols; both distract the people from the true God.

The objects and practices of false religion will be taken away. The people will have to go to Yahweh alone for consultation and advice since he is the only source of hope and salvation. Images and stone pillars consecrated to the Canaanite gods will have to be destroyed, for they produce only ruin (cf. Mic. 1:7). Asherim are singled out because they had a special appeal for the people on account of the fertility rites connected with them. In Canaanite religion Asherah was viewed as the wife of Baal. Sometimes the Israelites were tempted to conceive of her as the wife of Yahweh; therefore she was specially targeted for destruction.

Micah concludes this tirade and the whole section of chs. 4–5, turning once again to the nations he mentioned at the beginning (cf. 4:2). The nations that are not converted and do not join the universal pilgrimage to Zion, who do not want to join the era of faith and peace, will be treated like rebellious Israel.

THE JUDGMENT OF GOD
AND THE HOPE OF
RESTORATION
Micah 6:1–7:20

The last two chapters of the book of Micah are made up of a series of oracles of denunciation and salvation which seem to belong to a different hand from the rest of the book.

A. S. van der Woude and some of his followers have attempted to prove that chs. 6–7 were written by an Israelite prophet from the northern kingdom, also from the 8th cent. B.C. and possibly of the same name as his southern counterpart. Their principal arguments, taken collectively, make the hypothesis believable, although they do not present a tight case:

(1) Chs. 1–5 show the influence of Isaiah, while chs. 6–7 are more related to Hosea.

(2) Chs. 6–7 give geographical and historical names from the north, never speaking of Judah and Jerusalem.

(3) Chs. 1–5 underline the Zion traditions, while chs. 6–7 stress the northern traditions of the Exodus and the Conquest.

(4) Chs. 1–5 are addressed to the principal sectors of society (cf. 2:6; 3:5, 11), while chs. 6–7 speak to the people or to a city as a whole, and even when they speak to the leaders the vocabulary is different.

(5) The general introduction to the book (1:1) speaks of oracles for both the north and the south.

In answer to the preceding arguments and having in mind our exegesis of the preceding chapters, it must be pointed out that the influence of Isaiah on Micah is not as clear as once it was imagined, for Micah had a very independent personality and possibly a keener sense of justice. Also, although Jerusalem is not mentioned explicitly in the last two chapters, the city alluded to is most probably Jerusalem, whose walls have to be rebuilt (cf. 7:11). Besides, the two northern kings mentioned, Omri and Ahab (6:16), are the two best examples of the blatant injustice and unrestrained militarism so strongly condemned in the controversy with the false prophets (cf. 1 Kgs. 16:27-28; 20:1-43; 21:1-29). Likewise, the denunciations of Mic. 6–7 seem to be addressed to the same groups as those of chs. 2–3. One can also see in both sections the parallel contrast the prophet establishes between himself and his adversaries (cf. 3:8; 7:7).

Some authors attribute chs. 6–7 to Micah of Moresheth who, they think, also prophesied in the north, at least until the fall of Samaria, as was the case with Amos (cf. Amos 7:12-13). Thus the differences in vocabulary, traditions, and details would be due to the adaptation of the prophet to the different regions. Bruce Vawter notes that the contents of Mic. 6–7 fit well the era of Micah of Moresheth and that the formulae of traditional liturgical language used in the book were well known to the prophet (*Amos, Hosea, Micah*, 159); it could also be that they come from an editor connected with the temple worship.

Some commentators think that this section, particularly 6:1-8, does not belong to Micah because it is above what could be expected from the rustic Judahite they imagine that Micah was. Some others add that the language and style of these chapters belong to a later period, probably after the Babylonian Exile; Otto Eissfeldt believes that 7:8-20 refers to the fall of Samaria and not to the destruction of Jerusalem (*The Old Testament* [Oxford: Basil Blackwell and New York: Harper & Row, 1965], 412). Some have pointed out the references to the Covenant found in this section as well as the echoes of the vocabulary of Deuteronomy ("remember," "know," "recognize," "house of bondage," "ransom"); hence they see here contacts with an early source of Deuteronomy which could date back to Hezekiah's and Micah's time (cf. Deut. 5:6, 15; 6:9, 12, 25; 7:8, 9, 18; 8:2, 14, 18). The language and content of this section have been so structured by a final liturgical editorial hand that it is difficult to determine with precision the texts that could have come from the 8th cent. (cf. Mic. 6:9-15; 7:2-7; 7:11-13).

The last section of Micah is, then, commonly regarded as an editorial unit composed of several oracles structured in two parts under the general headings of denunciation and promises (6:1–7:7; 7:8-20). In line with Luis Alonso-Schökel, I prefer to see this section as a loose editorial unit under the theme "The Judgment of God" with three parts:

I. Prophetic *rib* ("litigation") and the appropriate response
   (6:1-8)
II. The sins of the people: injustice and disloyalty
    A. Absence of justice (6:9-16)
    B. Absence of loyalty (7:1-6)
III. Acceptance of punishment, confession of sin, and
     assurance of pardon (7:7-20)

The prophet opens the section with a prophetic *rib,* calling on
nature to witness the case of God against his people (6:1-3); the
historical events through which God had shown his mercy to Israel
are presented as a mild reproach to which the people respond with
a generous cultic ritual (6:4-5, 6-7). With a severe and lapidary
statement, the prophet recalls that the authentic way to God goes
through justice and loyalty, as was stressed from the early days of
the Covenant of Sinai (v. 8). When confronted with the lack of justice and loyalty, the people confess their sin and listen to liturgical
oracles and prayers for restoration and salvation.

The editorial hand of this section attempted to adapt its contents to the message of the first part of Micah. As we shall see in
the exegesis of the following verses, there is a clear homogeneity in
contents, and we find in a new and condensed form what had been
presented in chs. 2–5. The hopes announced in the early chapters
become the prayer of the concluding section of Micah.

PROPHETIC *RIB* OR LITIGATION (6:1-8)

The *rib* or legal litigation, which some consider an original composition of Micah of Moresheth, opens with a direct style full of tenderness, and presents what is considered a typical prophetic covenant
lawsuit between the two sides in the Covenant (cf. Amos 3:3-8;
Hos. 4:1-6). God has a strong case against his people because he
has done his part in the Covenant while the people have failed in
their most basic duties towards God and towards the poor. This *rib*
is not explicitly part of a wider penitential service ending in penance
and conversion (cf. Jer. 7:1-28; 11:1-17). It is, rather, an urgent and
intense appeal to a change of behavior followed by an implicit recognition of sin and a sincere attempt at expiation; it concludes with
the solemn "liturgical Torah" proclaiming God's code of holiness.
The text is well known for its use in the Good Friday liturgy.

The prophet opens the section with an invitation similar to the one found at the beginning of the book, introducing and summoning the witnesses. The process begins with a triple invitation to "hear" and a triple mention of the controversy that God has with his people. In Mic. 1:4 the mountains had a theophanic function revealing the presence of God, while in the text at hand the mountains and hills are juridical witnesses in a covenant legal lawsuit, not unlike those of pagan nations in which the gods of the two parties were called as witnesses. Their presence as silent witnesses gives solemnity to the process.

The mountains and hills are the best witnesses, because from their heights they have seen the sins of the people; their sins had often been committed in "the high places" (cf. 2 Kgs. 15:35; 16:4; 17:7-12; Isa. 36:7; Hos. 10:8; Amos 7:9). Also the prophet mentions together with the mountains and hills the "enduring foundations of the earth," the highest and the deepest (cf. Isa. 7:11), for they have experienced the hand of the LORD. The works of creation, as elsewhere in the OT, are presumed to have intelligence and to know the LORD. They are impartial, eternal, and sublime witnesses of his kindness. They are often the chosen places for the encounters of God with his people (Sinai, Nebo, Ebal, Gerizim, Zion, and Carmel).

God states his case to make Israel confront its ingratitude. The behavior of the people indicates that they have something against God. Thus God, instead of complaining and accusing the people, asks about their complaints against him who has shown nothing but love from the beginnings of their history as a nation.

The enumeration of the salvific acts of the people's history becomes the key for the accusation (cf. Isa. 1:2; Jer. 2:6-9; Hos. 11:1-12; 13:4-6; Amos 2:9-12): deliverance from Egypt, inspired leadership, salvation from their enemies, and entrance into the Promised Land. In spite of all the good the LORD has done, the people have failed to respond as expected. Amos 4:6-13, by way of contrast, enumerates the punishments that God has brought upon the people to make them come to their senses; all have been to no avail. God insistently demands an answer, but nobody seems to be listening; either they are asleep or they are not conscious of their sins. The people at times have complained that God has abandoned them, but in reality it is the people that have abandoned God.

God appears to seek historical evidence against himself; he examines his acts among his people. Like a father or a mother after the tragedy or the ungratefulness of a child God says: "After all I have done for them!"; "How did I fail?" (cf. Isa. 5:4); "Why did I receive such a reward after so much effort?" The prophet makes his point through a play with the sound of Hebrew words that helps to fix it in the minds of his listeners.

The text has a vocabulary often found in Deuteronomy and recalls the traditions of Num. 22–24; 1 Sam. 12:6; and Deut. 5:6. God had showed his providence and saved his people repeatedly through the human leadership he had provided. Moses and Aaron are mentioned together as in many biblical texts (cf. Josh. 24:5; 1 Sam. 12:8; Ps. 77:21; 105:26). Miriam is remembered as the prophetess of Exodus who sang of the divine liberation (cf. Exod. 15:20). Balaam seems to have been a prominent figure in legends which were popular in Micah's time. Shittim and Gilgal possibly recall the miraculous events of the crossing of the river Jordan, but the reference is not clear and the text is defective.

God wants his people to remember and recognize "the saving acts of the LORD" through which he showed his fidelity to the Covenant. God is to be acknowledged religiously as the savior who delivered his people from the unjust oppression of Egypt and from every difficulty they had faced throughout their history.

6-8   The prophet, with heavy satire, puts on the lips of the sinful people an appropriate and superficial answer that seeks to avoid true conversion. They answer God who had questioned himself by, in turn, questioning themselves. The question of the people is an implicit recognition of guilt. The prophet links together the themes of the reconciliation of sinners, the true nature of worship, and the demands God makes of people. Does God prefer worship over justice? This question is often raised in the Prophets (cf. Isa. 1:10-17; 29:13-14; 58:1-8; Jer. 6:20; Hos. 6:6; Joel 2:13; Amos 5:21-27; Zech. 7:4-6). The divine answer will climax in Mic. 6:8, the most basic verse in the whole book of Micah.

The question of the people is reminiscent of temple liturgies and the requirements needed to approach the altar of the LORD (cf. Ps. 15:2-5; Isa. 33:14-16). What does the LORD require from those who come to him? Micah points out that there is something worse than appearing before the LORD empty-handed (cf. Exod. 23:15;

34:20), namely appearing before him dirty-handed and empty-hearted, without justice.

God does not need sacrifices (cf. Ps. 50:12). He rejects them when they pretend to substitute for more basic social and religious duties. The cult and the temple could become a distraction, an opiate, and an obstacle to true conversion. External rites are valid only when they are an expression of internal convictions and not just empty and meaningless ritual.

The people show their initial conversion by trying to reestablish friendship with God through the means with which they are familiar, namely cultic sacrifices and offerings. The intensity of the people's desire to win God's favor is well expressed in the growing order of the sacrifices mentioned. The people seem to think of God as a king who has to be bought or appeased through the payment of an increasing tribute or bribe. The people is aware of its nothingness and of the greatness of "God on high."

Israel does not know the only authentic way to "come before the LORD," which is total personal conversion. True religion was not going to allow persons to commit sins and let the animals pay the price, anymore than it would permit sins to be expiated with holy water or lighted votive candles. The people thought that burnt offerings (where *everything* was dedicated to the LORD) demanded no personal involvement of the one offering them: a year-old calf was a fitting sacrifice for sin (cf. Lev. 9:3); a thousand rams and "rivers of oil" could be a reminder of Solomon's generous sacrifices (cf. 1 Kgs. 8:62-66; cf. also 3:4; 2 Chr. 30:24; 35:7); human sacrifices are mentioned at the end as a climax. Human sacrifices were a pagan custom that had come to influence the social and religious life of Israel; the practice implied a renunciation of all the hopes and dreams placed especially in the firstborn as a blessing from the LORD. It was believed that in desperate cases the divinity demanded human victims as a condition to obtain deliverance (cf. Jer. 19:5; 32:35; cf. Lev. 18:21; 20:2). But God does not want victims. He hates the very idea of human victims of any kind. God does not want sacrifices except the sacrifice of self through the life of justice, so that no person will be sacrificed or victimized. The most expensive and elaborate worship cannot compensate for the lack of justice.

8　The answer of God is presented in solemn and universal terms:

> He has showed you, O man, what is good;
> and what does the LORD require of you
> but to do justice, and to love kindness,
> and to walk humbly with your God? (Mic. 6:8)

Scholars generally attribute this important verse to Micah of Moresheth, since a similar teaching is found in Micah's contemporaries; some attribute it to an anonymous prophet either from the 8th cent. or from the postexilic period. A few have thought of the period of Manasseh, Hezekiah's son, especially because the context makes allusion to human sacrifices (cf. 2 Kgs. 21:6).

The questions raised by the people have already revealed doubts about the sufficiency of a purely external and ritual religion. The prophet now answers as an interpreter of God's will, stressing that true religion crystallizes its value through the moral life that accompanies it. God is served not through sacrifices and offerings but through an inner religious life made manifest through humility before God and through mercy towards one's neighbor. This was the essence of the Covenant which had been condensed in the Ten Commandments.

God wants service expressed principally in the practice of love and justice. Sacrifices are, at best, symbols or sacraments of self-surrender to God; otherwise they are just empty and meaningless religiosity. God does not want from the worshipper quality of *things,* but quality of *life;* the life of the worshipper is far more important than the acts of worship. In the NT Jesus will stress true worship and inner religion, announcing a worship in spirit and in truth, with a perfect harmony between the interior disposition (spirit) and the external actions through which it is *verified* and becomes effectively true.

The prophet enumerates three qualities which describe the most important aspects of one general disposition that might be called "holiness": *to do or practice justice, to love kindness,* and *to walk humbly with God.* Thus Micah has put down in a concise manner a synthesis of the doctrine of Amos, Hosea, and Isaiah. Amos had proposed the demands of justice over sacrifices; Hosea had emphasized the importance of tenderness and love; and Isaiah had stressed faith and obedience to God (cf. Amos 5:24; Hos. 6:6; Isa. 7:9; 30:15).

The prophetic injunction is addressed to "man"; the word can be read as a personification of Israel or as a human being in subordination to God. The term "man" serves to generalize and universalize the scope of the divine directive.

The practice of *justice* required of Israel, in the mind of Micah and of other prophets, is more than a simple obedience of the social and ritual religious obligations derived from the Law. It implies a commitment and a responsibility for the defense of the poor and the powerless so that they will not be victimized by the more powerful groups of society.

The loving-kindness and fidelity of God throughout the history of the people is the model and pattern for the *loving mercy (hesed)* that the prophets demand from Israel. It is generally associated with the Exodus and the Covenant. More than human feelings, loving mercy includes compassion and steadfast and loyal love, such as exist among the members of the same clan, tribe, and family. Loving mercy is a community-oriented activity, expressed concretely by protecting and helping those in need and through a spirit of solidarity (cf. Num. 14:18; Ps. 86:15; 103:8; 145:8; Joel 2:13).

Israel must "walk humbly with God." Adam, Noah, Abraham, and others had "walked with God" (cf. Gen. 3:8; 6:9), and God had walked with all his people in the Exodus. He had shown himself watchful and attentive to the needs of the people, listening to the cries of their heart. The people must listen to the heart of God and his desire for mercy and compassion for those in need. God does not want the people simply to come to him but actually to walk with him, seeing things through his own eyes and behaving towards the poor in the same saving manner as he had done in their history. Humility is a virtue required in walking with God, in being faithful and attentive servants of the LORD (cf. Ps. 123:2). The people must pay attention primarily to the interests of God and to the interests of the poor. This humility is in direct opposition to the pride and presumption that drives persons to be self-centered and closed to everyone else.

In Mic. 6:8 the prophet has presented a perfect summary of the biblical religion found frequently in the Prophets. True religion must be a means for an encounter with God and with others, and must not become an end in itself and for itself. Love in its fullness is the only valid foundation for all human and divine relationships.

THE SIN OF THE PEOPLE: ABSENCE OF JUSTICE (6:9-16)

The prophet has just solemnly proclaimed that, rather than ritual worship, the LORD requires his people to practice justice, love kindness, and walk humbly with him. The road to God has become eroded for the people of Judah and Jerusalem because of the basic lack of justice which the prophet now denounces. This section reminds us of Isa. 5:1-24 where, after remembering the favors and expectations of God for his people, the prophet contends that God has found in their midst only crime and exploitation of every kind.

This section is characterized by serious textual difficulties not easily solved, although the general meaning of the passage is quite clear. The prophet denounces concrete and specific forms of injustice and announces a fitting punishment. Scholars have tried to change the order of the verses and omit some lines to make the text more understandable, but every change gives rise to difficulties greater than the ones it solves. The prophet, echoing themes of Mic. 2:1-11 and 3:1-4, makes a passionate and rhetorical indictment of the injustices of daily life.

Micah denounces here the urban practices of apparently insignificant commercial frauds through which the poor were effectively robbed. The city, Jerusalem, is addressed directly as a center of political, judicial, and economic power. The capital city provided the models of exploitation for other towns and villages in the region. Although such practices were also common in the neighboring countries, it is in Israel only that the cries for justice for the poor are heard with intensity.

The prophet opens with a brief enumeration of commercial crimes (6:10-12), and passes on to announce the appropriate punishments, which are patterned after the "futility curses" often associated with the breach of the Covenant (vv. 13-15; cf. Lev. 26:14-26). The section ends with an editorial summary that betrays a postexilic hand (Mic. 6:16).

The text of v. 9 presents some difficulties since the speaker is not easily identified. The message is addressed to the "tribe and assembly of the city," with a possible allusion to the liturgical feasts and gatherings that periodically took place in Jerusalem (cf. Isa. 33:20); the words of the prophet seem to have a national audience in mind. While the people gather to celebrate and forget the problems of life, the prophet thinks of taking the opportunity to make them uncomfortable by reminding them of their social inequities. The crimes and frauds through which some enriched themselves (Mic. 6:10-12) are all well attested by contemporary prophets (cf. Hos. 12:7; Amos 8:5; also Ezek 45:9-12; Lev. 19:35-36; Deut. 25:13-16; Prov. 11:1; 20:10, 23). The lack of official national standards for weights and measures as well as the influence of international commerce, for which measures with the same names but with different values were used in each region, favored a confusing diversity of measures that worked effectively against the poor. Through the use of false weights and measures the price of food was easily inflated so that the workers were deprived of the true value of their wages.

The rich are seen principally as thieves who, with an external show of piety, practice violence and deceit; their treasures and possessions are the fruit of violence (cf. Mic. 2:1-2, 8-10; 3:2-3, 10; Jer. 22:3; Amos 3:9-10; 6:4-6). The tenant farmers and the poor in general were most often victimized since they had to pay their debts in kind with the fruits of the land and also give their share to the rich landholders; ephah-measures of wicker baskets, which stretched easily and thus increased the amount they could contain, were a curse for the poor. Lev. 19:35-36 places together injustice in the tribunals with cheating in commercial deals; Micah in the first section (Mic. 2:1-5; 3:1-3, 9-12) condemns in the strongest terms the cruel abuse of power, the injustices and expropriations which were carried out "legally" in the tribunals of justice. This present section condemns the no less tragic forms of exploitation quietly taking place every day, economic frauds through which the poor were being gradually and effectively bled to death. The culprits are the rich and the "inhabitants" or, better, the upper classes of urban society, including the princes, judges, and other leaders; they made victims out of most of the little people.

The daily "violence" that reigns in the land has created such a hopeless situation that only a devastating deluge, often in the form of a military invasion, will be able to do away with it and pave the way for a new order; as "in the days of old," "now the earth was corrupt in God's sight, and the earth was filled with violence. And God saw the earth, and behold, it was corrupt; for all flesh had corrupted their way upon the earth" (Gen. 6:11-12; cf. Mic. 6:14; 3:12).

The appropriate punishment is announced in the form of futility curses which frustrate the efforts and goals of the oppressors (cf. Lev. 26:14-16; Deut. 27:11-26; 28:15-68; Josh. 8:34; Amos 5:11-12); their labors will prove to be fruitless. They shall eat but not be satisfied; rather, they will experience pain "in their guts" (the Syriac Version of the Bible sees here an allusion to some form of indigestion or dysentery). The hopes of sowing will be accompanied by despair in harvesting. They will have no oil, which was so basic for the daily life of Orientals, for anointing, perfumes, cooking, and even for religious rites. They shall not drink wine, a source of warmth, joy, and blessing. The prophet implies that the rich merchants who cheat are also the owners of the fields, hence their injustice in commercial deals is punished with agricultural disasters.

The punishment section begins with an emphatic "I," which contrasts with the triple "you" that follows. God "has begun" something which can only intensify and punish more deeply. Possibly, the first skirmishes of an incipient war were seen as an omen of what was to come. Since they have cut their real ties with God, they have no hope for the future. God takes the initiative in a punishment that will culminate in total ruin and desolation.

Some scholars have suggested that the references to desolation and deliverance of the people to the sword (Mic. 6:13-14, 16) are editorial allusions to the destruction of Jerusalem by the Babylonians in 586 B.C., since similar terminology is also found in Jeremiah and Ezekiel. If this is the case, then the final redactor of the book of Micah may have wanted to establish a connection between the Exile in Babylon and the daily injustices in commerce and trade.

The oracle ends with an editorial recapitulation of what precedes, summarized in an accusation and a judgment. Jerusalem is no better than her sister Samaria, in whose steps she follows and from whom she has learned to do evil (cf. 1:5; Ezek. 23:1-49). Already at the time of Micah's writing, as it would be in later times, it was a deep insult to compare Jerusalem with Samaria, especially when the Jews claimed to follow the LORD and to learn from him alone.

The models of Jerusalem's behavior are the two most notorious kings of the north, for the root of the sin of Jerusalem was in Samaria (Mic. 1:5). King Omri had left a lasting memory for his great military exploits as well as for the construction of a new capital, the city of Samaria (1 Kgs. 16:23-28). King Ahab was a notorious symbol of idol worship, social injustice, and great construction projects; he was even better remembered for his criminal usurpation of the vineyard of Naboth (cf. 21:1-29). Both kings had probably tolerated unfair commercial practices through which some citizens became richer and so helped pay for the military expenses. Their construction and military activities, as those of Jerusalem, had been built on blood and were doomed to destruction.

THE SIN OF THE PEOPLE: ABSENCE OF LOYALTY (7:1-7)

The prophet had solemnly stated in Mic. 6:8 that God wants the practice of justice and love of kindness; this kindness is expressed in generosity, respect, truthfulness, and fidelity that build up community and solidarity through the mutual commitment of the members of the community. After showing that there is no justice, the prophet goes on to denounce such basic lack of loyalty that makes peaceful social life totally impossible. Alienation, isolation, suspicion, and loneliness are the by-products of the injustice that pervades social relations. Sin produces its own punishment. One can see in this section one of the most pessimistic pictures of a social situation that can be found in the Old Testament.

The prophet opens with a lamentation on the general situation and then zeroes in on particular issues, especially on the family and friends. In the first part of the book (chs. 2–3) Micah had denounced the corruption of public officials; now he shows that everyone is caught up in the web of injustice. No one can be trusted. It is a disgrace to have to live in such bad times, since where falsehood and deceit are rampant the mutual trust needed for human relations has been uprooted.

The situation presented by the prophet has close parallels in Egyptian and Assyrian texts, as some scholars have pointed out. In the OT, because there are so many allusions to this type of situation, the complaints seem more rhetorical than historical (cf. Isa. 59:3-4; Ps. 12:1-2; 14:2-3; 55:9-14, 20-21). As in the preceding verse (Mic. 6:16), we could also read in this section a reference to the conditions in Israel during the reign of King Ahab and the ministry of the prophet Elijah, a period when everyone is described as a sinner (cf. 1 Kgs. 19:10, 14). Isa. 5:1-7 seems to refer to a similar situation of universal prevarication. Jeremiah speaks of a parallel tragedy immediately before the Babylonian Exile (cf. Jer. 5:1-5; 8:22–9:6). As in the days of Sodom and Gomorrah, the perversion is so generalized that it is impossible to single out one good person in the land.

This section returns to some of the literary traits of the first chapters of the book. The prophet uses assonance, rhyme, and alliteration. The first and the last verses (Mic. 7:1, 7) form a literary inclusion with a speaker in the first person in both verses. Some commentators divide this section in two parts (vv. 1-4 and 5-7), while others try to set the verses in a new and more logical order (vv. 3, 5, 6, 4). The general sense is clear, for it repeats eloquently that

> They have all gone astray, they are all alike corrupt;
>> there is none that does good,
>> no, not one. (Ps. 14:3)

The prophet pours out the loneliness, pain, and anguish of his heart to the LORD in bitter lamentation, hoping that the eyes and ears of the people will finally open. Salvation will have to come from above or from the outside, since within the society itself no healthy elements are left. The prophet portrays himself as a poor man who has entered a field to collect the gleanings after the harvest. He is hungry and hopes to find some leftover fruits, but his hope is foiled. The fruits sought for are loyal actions springing from a social and moral system based on justice (cf. Isa. 5:1-7; John 15:1-8; Mark 11:12-14, 20-22). The prophet, in a way, is the first victim of his own mission; he is caught up in God and expresses God's suffering. His mission is not just to bring sin to light but to achieve a conversion which, tragically, is impossible.

There is not a single good and upright person left in the land. Moral standards are universally disregarded, and the spirit of mercy and compassion has been extinguished. No one loves his neighbor. Everyone is a Cain for his brother (cf. Gen. 4:9); they are worthy descendants of Jacob, who had been an expert at deceiving his family, even his own brother and father (cf. Gen. 25:28-34; 27:1-36; 30:25-43; Hos. 12:2-9). All have become inhuman, like animals, devoid of feelings for others (cf. Pss. 1, 14).

The most inhuman exploiters are those persons who hold political, judicial, and economic power (cf. Mic. 3:1-4, 9-12). They are good only at doing evil; that is their specialty. They have led the way along the path of corruption and love of money which has resulted in the present chaotic social situation. The powerful man "utters the evil desire of his soul" (7:3) and sets in motion a process in which crimes are woven together, capturing all his allies, friends, and neighbors in the web of his crime. Such was the case of King Ahab who, by expressing his desire for the vineyard of Naboth, had inspired the scheming Queen Jezebel to write letters to the elders and nobles who dwelt with Naboth in his city; they selected two false witnesses so Naboth could be stoned to death by all the townspeople (1 Kgs. 21:1-29). Everyone was involved and shared in the crimes set in motion by the king; some of the common people might even have participated in the stoning of Naboth without being aware that it was the culmination of a criminal conspiracy. Micah sees that human lives are sacrificed in the interests of money and greed. Neither the interests of God nor those of the poor are of any account. A rugged individualism reigns, producing fruits of death.

The prophet describes the situation graphically with two images from the agricultural realm: the best of the powerful is as crooked as a brier, and the most upright among them is like a thorn hedge ready to scratch a confident passerby (cf. Mic. 2:8). Since the path of justice has been closed by the briers and thorns of injustice, suffering and utter confusion are in store for everyone.

Sin and injustice create their own punishment (7:5-7). They produce a calamitous rupture in human relations. The prophet laments a situation where no one can be trusted, not even those persons with whom one has established more intimate bonds: neighbor, friend, spouse. "Do not trust a friend" was probably a proverb then, as it is still in Spanish. When money becomes the idol of society and determines human relationships, then everything and everyone has a price; nothing is sacred, and everything can be sacrificed. Everyone is at war with everybody else. A person's enemies are even those of his own household. The real bases of society have been eroded, once there is no trust, loyalty, and respect for others. The rugged individualism that has taken over produces hostility and inhumanity towards others and deep loneliness within individuals.

Micah's language and style in these verses, along the lines of a rhetorical or wisdom lamentation and exhortation, is full of es-

chatological overtones which are picked up by Jesus in the Gospels
(cf. Matt. 10:35-36; Mark 13:12; Luke 12:53). We find similar
oracles in the Prophets as well as in the Psalms (cf. Ps. 54:5-24),
stating that life is impossible when the principles of justice and
trust are disregarded:

> Let every one beware of his neighbor,
>   and put no trust in any brother;
> for every brother is a supplanter,
>   and every neighbor goes about as a slanderer.
> Every one deceives his neighbor,
>   and no one speaks the truth;
> they have taught their tongue to speak lies;
>   they commit iniquity and are too weary to repent.
> Heaping oppression upon oppression, and deceit upon deceit,
>   they refuse to know me, says the LORD. (Jer. 9:4-6)

While the pillars of social life are falling down and no one can
be trusted, the prophet affirms his own faith in the fidelity of
God: "But as for me, I will look to the LORD, I will wait for the
God of my salvation; my God will hear me" (Mic. 7:7). When
one cannot trust in people, the only way out is to trust in the
LORD. The prophet, as in 3:8, establishes a contrast between
himself and his hearers. When external religion and institutions
are falling, then his own personal faith becomes his strength.
Even when a situation may seem humanly hopeless and God
chooses to remain silent, there is no room for desperation or
cynicism, for "the LORD is good to those who wait for him, to
the soul that seeks him. It is good that one should wait quietly
for the salvation of the LORD" (Lam. 3:25-26). One can always
hope against hope. When it becomes too painful to look at the
present, the prophet takes time out to look at the future to
kindle his hope. The fidelity of God is the guarantee of a future
restoration.

Some scholars consider Mic. 7:7 as a possible conclusion of the
work of Micah. The section that follows then is considered to have
been added after the Babylonian Exile. But the contents of this
verse can be easily linked with the preceding and the following sections. It seems more probable that it marks a conclusion of the section on absence of loyalty, forming a literary inclusion with v. 1. In
this section a contrast is established between the prophet and the
untrustworthy society in which he lives.

ACCEPTANCE OF PUNISHMENT, CONFESSION OF SIN, AND ASSURANCE OF PARDON (7:8-20)

The last section of the book of Micah seems to be of cultic origin and is permeated with ideas of hope and the certainty of salvation. God's anger and punishments are only temporary; there is compassion in his anger. The light of dawn follows even the darkest night.

The situation underlying this last section is different from that of the preceding verses: the people have fallen in defeat (Mic. 7:8) and the city has lost its walls (v. 11); a portion of the inhabitants are still in captivity, while others are in the land of Judah (vv. 13-14). The text does not convey any idea of threat or punishment but seems to give just a calm description of a present reality. There is no explicit oracle of deliverance, although there is a profound hope of restoration and salvation. In the midst of a present pessimism, the writer sees reasons for an exuberant optimism rooted in God.

After Hermann Gunkel, this section is commonly regarded as a concluding prophetic liturgy, not unlike the liturgies found in the Psalms (cf. Pss. 12; 27:1-6; 44; 50; 62; 75; 77; 80; 81; 82; 90; 95). There are four distinct liturgical "moments" or parts in Micah.

(1) 7:8-10   Acknowledgment of sin and hope of deliverance
(2) 7:11-13   Oracle of restoration and liberation
(3) 7:14-17   Hope-filled community prayer
(4) 7:18-20   Hymn of praise and hope in the LORD

These four parts are a reminder of the various elements included in liturgical forms and of the different participants in the temple rites: the people in general, the prophetic voice (of priests or prophets), a chosen group of singers, and a congregation attending the ceremony. As is common in the liturgy, especially as reflected in the Psalms, we find allusions to the Covenant, petitions that accompany lamentations, and expressions of praise and hope. Salvation will include the elements dreamed of after the Exile: the trampling upon enemies, the reconstruction of the city walls, and the gathering of the dispersed tribes of Israel. The period after the Babylonian Captivity offers a perfect life setting for this section, although some commentators have thought of the fall of Samaria or of a partial destruction of Jerusalem before the Exile as possible contexts.

In a new light and from a new perspective, we find for the last time some of the themes that have been presented repeatedly in Micah: the pitiful condition of the people suffering at the hands of enemies, promises of restoration, and the king-shepherd leading the people. The perspective now is exclusively one of pardon and hope.

Acknowledgment of Sin and Hope of Deliverance (7:8-10)

Jerusalem, the city personified, speaks to her enemies in a language similar to that found in the book of Lamentations (cf. Lam. 1:18-22). The city has fallen and sits in darkness like a prisoner of war, but she hopes that the light of the LORD, his saving justice, will shine again on her. She looks to a new Exodus that will bring her from darkness into light. The LORD will come to the rescue because he makes as his own the cause and the plight of his people, particularly when they are in need. The fate of Jerusalem is not in the hands of her enemies but in the hands of her God. He will deliver Jerusalem and will humble the pride of the oppressor. The enemy addressed by the city is probably Edom, the southern neighbor allied with Babylon in the destruction of Jerusalem (cf. Ps. 137:7; Amos 1:11-12); Edom had become the classic and typical enemy of Israel (cf. Obad. 11-14; Isa. 34:5-17; Ezek. 25:12-14; 35:1-15).

Jerusalem under judgment considers herself as a poor person in need of a protector to defend her from a powerful enemy. The city acknowledges her sin, and like the son in the Parable of the Prodigal Son recognizes that "I have sinned against him" (Mic. 7:9; cf. Luke 15:18). One can see in Jerusalem's resignation her acceptance of the divine retribution, submission to God's will, and hope for salvation. The LORD is no longer a threatening figure but a saving and merciful God who will rise above human failure. The LORD is expected to act for his own sake, since a conquered people was a sign of a conquered and fallen God.

The enemy will be vanquished and trodden down according to the custom of putting the foot of the conqueror upon the neck of the defeated adversary. But the main enemy to be utterly defeated is internal injustice and sin: "He will tread our iniquities under foot. Thou wilt cast all our sins into the depths of the sea" (Mic. 7:19). God will show in the end the true colors of his justice; he will justify himself by saving his people. Her enemies will then experience the present fate of Jerusalem over which they now rejoice.

Oracle of Restoration and Liberation (7:11-13)

This oracle, part of a prophetic liturgy of hope, dates possibly from the Persian period (after 538 B.C.), when the return from exile and the reconstruction of Jerusalem became a reality. The language of this section has eschatological overtones which may not be interpreted chronologically. "In that day," "a day" (Mic. 7:12, 11) of prophetic expectation is announced after the acknowledgment of sin and the acceptance of punishment. After true repentance there is room only for mercy and hope. Life will go on, and things will return to normal; the Exile will come to an end, and the people will live securely in the land. The rebuilt walls of the city will contribute to a physical, social, and religious sense of peace. Since the boundaries will be extended, the enemies will be far away. The divine promise is personalized and intensified with a triple repetition of "you": *your* walls and *your* boundaries will be remade, and all peoples will come to *you*.

Streams of people will come to Jerusalem (cf. 4:1-2; 2:12); the author seems to be thinking here of the return of the Jewish exiles and refugees. If he were thinking of foreigners coming to Jerusalem, it would be difficult to understand why their land would become desolate and they would be trodden down, unless the language is just part of the eschatological and apocalyptic tone of this section. The name and influence of Jerusalem will be similar to that of the time of Solomon when the borders of Israel were extended from sea to sea (east to west) and from mountain to mountain (north to south). The four corners of the earth will look up to Jerusalem, which will be the salvific center of the world.

While Jerusalem will be rebuilt and repopulated, the world of those who reject conversion will be desolate. The salvation of Zion will be accompanied by the judgment of her enemies. The author of this isolated verse (7:14) is probably thinking of the neighboring peoples of Judah who actively resisted the reconstruction of the city and made life miserable for the returned exiles (cf. Ezra 4:1-22; Neh. 2:19-20; 4:1-23). Those who do not wish to be part of the saving plan of God will fall under his avenging justice and will be barren and desolate.

Hope-filled Community Prayer (7:14-17)

The response of the community to the salvific prophecy of Mic. 7:11-13 is a hope-filled prayer, similar to those prayers raised in times of national disgrace (cf. Joel 2:17; Isa. 63:15–64:12). God is asked to repeat the salvation events in the history of the people, making alive again the hopes and miracles that accompanied the Exodus from Egypt and the Conquest of the Promised Land. Later prophetic texts will repeat this theme in a new light, promising a new and more glorious Exodus as well as a new covenant in which there will be no room for the failures and infidelities that accompanied the first one (cf. Isa. 41:17-20; 43:16-21; 48:20-22; 55:3-5; Jer. 31:1-22, 31-34; Ezek. 36:24-36). The prophetic writer of the early postexilic period realized that in their own time a new exodus was actually taking place.

The prayer asks God to be the shepherd of Israel, pasturing his people as in the days of old. "Shepherd" was a title commonly applied to kings in the ancient Near East. God is to exercise his kingship in the loving and provident manner in which a shepherd cares for his flock. The author of the prayer has in mind the pilgrimage of the people through the desert under God's guidance, although in alluding to Mic. 5:4 one could see here a reference to Davidic times.

The people are said to be God's "inheritance," a sacred and precious possession which one must keep, protect, and defend; it has been passed down from generation to generation well preserved and improved. The people returning from captivity found themselves in a hostile environment and prayed for the peace and abundance of Bashan and Gilead, lands famous for their rich pastures. The peoples recognized that the actions of God were the determining factor in their history. They expect God to save now as he saved before (cf. Exod. 13:21; 33:14; 2 Sam. 5:24). He is faithful to his own saving actions in history.

The second part of the prayer (Mic. 7:16-17) focuses attention on the nations. The power of the LORD overcomes the power of the nations; they are ashamed and become impotent when confronted with the power of God (cf. Zech. 4:6). Those who are haughty and proud will become speechless and numb, astonished in admiration according to a common prophetic theme (cf. Mic. 4:1-2, 13; 5:6; Job 21:5; 29:9; 40:4).

While in the early part of Micah nations were said to come to the LORD, attracted by the law and justice of Jerusalem (cf. Mic. 4:1-4), now they are said to be drawn by fear. Those whose land will become desolate (cf. 7:13) will seek a new land, one of law and justice under the guidance of God. The nations (evil political and social powers) will be conquered and humiliated like the serpent cursed in Gen. 3:14-15; their humiliation, after the previous humiliation of Israel, and the acceptance of justice will pave the way for a new world of peace and justice, and for a return to a paradisiacal condition on earth.

Hymn of Praise and Hope in the LORD (7:18-20)

The prophecy of Micah closes with a short but magnificent hymn extolling the greatness of God. Numerous scholars think that this hymn contains the greatest doxology found in the Old Testament. The hymn has echoes in numerous texts in the Bible (cf. Exod. 34:6; Neh. 9:17; Ps. 86:15; 103:8; 145:8; Jonah 4:2).

The writer makes a pun on Micah's own name, "Who is like Yahweh," in order to sing the magnificence of God. The LORD is great, not so much because of his awe-inspiring and spectacular deeds in nature and in history, but because of his total victory over sin and transgression, and because of his loving mercy through which he proves his fidelity to his promises. The justice or "anger" of God is not inflexible and heartless, since he delights in steadfast love. His very nature inclines him to pardon much more than the repentance of the sinner merits. God has never changed. He does not change his plans because of the resistance of sinners. The power of goodness in the end overcomes all evil. In the NT, in line with the OT prophetic wisdom, the power and the goodness of God will be revealed to such a point that he will draw salvation and goodness out of the suffering and death of his Chosen One (cf. John 3:16; 11:51-52; Rom. 8:28).

The prophet makes an impressive enumeration of the various manifestations of God's mercy; four statements in the present tense and four in the future are summed up in the final stanza illustrating God's fidelity to his promises.

- He pardons iniquity.
- He passes over transgressions.
- He does not retain his anger for ever.

- He delights in steadfast love.
- He will again have compassion.
- He will tread our iniquities under foot.
- He will cast all our sins into the depths of the sea.
- He will show faithfulness and steadfast love.

Micah's last statement stressing God's fidelity to his promises as he had "sworn to our fathers from the days of old" (Mic. 7:20) is the key to understanding all the statements about God's merciful and compassionate love.

God has shown his divine power in the punishment of Jerusalem, but he will show a different and greater power in pardoning and eliminating sin from the world. He will pass over transgressions as a traveler who does not pay attention to the distractions and things he sees along a road. He will overlook iniquity out of love for the humble remnant of his inheritance which is sacred to his love.

God will deal with sins as with a conquered enemy, treading iniquities under foot. Sins will be cast into the depths of the sea and like the Egyptians, the old enemies of Israel, they will drown in the sea. The conquest of sin will be total and final; from then on only goodness and mercy will triumph and flourish. This same idea is presented elsewhere in Scripture under the image of taking away and burying sins, as one buries a corpse (cf. Ps. 32:1; 103:12). When sin is taken away and is out of sight, then the mercy and goodness of God will reign on earth.

The concluding verse of Micah anchors in history the certainty of God's pardon and mercy. God will carry through to perfection the plan he started with the patriarchs—a plan to form a people of his own, according to his own heart. Christians see this plan brought to perfection in Jesus of Nazareth, as Mary spoke in the Magnificat quoting this verse of Micah (cf. Luke 1:55). The promises of God given to the patriarchs are still valid and will live forever in their descendants. Hope undying is the last word of Micah.

CONCLUSION

The challenges and the hopes of Micah do not belong to the past. They are not dead history. They belong to us, and we have to make them alive for our world. We have to look at the best of our past history and see how we can transform it into a source of dynamism to build international peace and unity. Micah dreamed of taking away political boundaries and religious divisions among the nations. The binding ties of justice and love are those that will build true unity in our world. That is our hope and our challenge.

SELECTED BIBLIOGRAPHY

Allen, Leslie C. *The Books of Joel, Obadiah, Jonah and Micah.* New International Commentary on the Old Testament (Grand Rapids: Wm. B. Eerdmans and London: Hodder and Stoughton, 1976).

Alonso-Schökel, Luis, and Sicre Diaz, José Luis. *Profetas,* 2 vols. (Madrid: Ediciones Cristiandad, 1980).

Bright, John. *A History of Israel,* 3rd ed. (Philadelphia: Westminster and London: SCM, 1981).

Brueggemann, Walter. "'Vine and Fig Tree': A Case Study in Imagination and Criticism," *Catholic Biblical Quarterly* 43 (1981): 188-204.

Burkitt, Frederik Crawfoot. "Micah 6 and 7 a Northern Prophecy," *Journal of Biblical Literature* 45 (1926): 159-161.

Carroll, Robert P. *When Prophecy Failed: Reactions and Responses to Failure in the Old Testament Prophetic Traditions* (London: SCM and New York: Seabury, 1979)

Heschel, Abraham Joshua. *The Prophets* (New York and London: Harper & Row, 1962).

Hillers, Delbert R. *Micah.* Hermeneia (Philadelphia: Fortress and London: SCM, 1984).

————. *Treaty-Curses and the Old Testament Prophets.* Biblica et Orientalia 16 (Rome: Pontifical Biblical Institute, 1964).

Kaufmann, Yeḥezkel. *The Religion of Israel from Its Beginnings to the Babylonian Exile* (Chicago: University of Chicago, 1960).

King, P. J. "Micah," in *The Jerome Biblical Commentary,* ed. Raymond E. Brown, Joseph A. Fitzmyer, and Roland E. Murphy (Englewood Cliffs: Prentice-Hall and London: Geoffrey Chapman, 1968), 283-289.

Lescow, Theodor. "Redaktionsgeschichtliche Analyse von Micah

1-5," *Zeitschrift für die alttestamentliche Wissenschaft* 84 (1972): 46-85.

Limburg, James. *The Prophets and the Powerless* (Atlanta: John Knox, 1976).

Lindblom, Christian Johannes. *Prophecy in Ancient Israel* (Philadelphia: Fortress and Oxford: Basil Blackwell, 1962).

Mays, James L. *Micah*. Old Testament Library (Philadelphia: Westminster and London: SCM, 1976).

Miranda, Jose P. *Marx and the Bible: A Critique of Philosophy of Oppression* (Maryknoll: Orbis, 1974).

von Rad, Gerhard. *The Message of the Prophets* (New York: Harper & Row and London: SCM, 1972).

Sicre, José Luis. *'Con los pobres de la tierra': La justicia social en los profetas de Israel* (Madrid: Ediciones Cristiandad, 1984).

————. *Los dioses olvidados*. Estudios de Antiguo Testamento (Madrid: Ediciones Cristiandad, 1979).

Tamez, Elsa. *Bible of the Oppressed* (Maryknoll: Orbis, 1982).

Vawter, Bruce. *Amos, Hosea, Micah*. Old Testament Message 7 (Wilmington: Michael Glazier and Dublin: Gill & Macmillan, 1981).

Willis, John T. "The Structure of Micah 3-5 and the Function of Micah 5:9-14 in the Book," *Zeitschrift für die alttestamentliche Wissenschaft* 81 (1969): 191-214.

Wilson, Robert R. *Prophecy and Society in Ancient Israel* (Philadelphia: Fortress, 1980).

Wolff, Hans Walter. *Micah the Prophet* (Philadelphia: Fortress, 1981).

van der Woude, Adam Simon. "Deutero-Micah: Ein Prophet aus Nord-Israel?" *Nederlands Theologisch Tijdschrift* 25 (1971): 365-378.

————. "Micah in Dispute with the Pseudo-prophets," *Vetus Testamentum* 19 (1969): 244-260.